D0952414

Empowered
LEADERS

Empowered

THE TEN PRINCIPLES OF CHRISTIAN LEADERSHIP

LEADERS

Hans FINZEL

CHARLES R. SWINDOLL, GENERAL EDITOR

WORD PUBLISHING

NASHVILLE

A Thomas Nelson Company

EMPOWERED LEADERS
Swindoll Leadership Library

Published in association with Dallas Theological Seminary (DTS):

General Editor: Charles Swindoll
Managing Editor: Roy B. Zuck

The theological opinions expressed by the author are not necessarily the
official position of Dallas Theological Seminary.

Library of Congress Cataloging-in-Publication Data

Finzel, Hans
Empowered leaders : a leader's work / by Hans Finzel
p.   cm.
Includes bibliographical references and index.

ISBN 0-8499-1362-4

1. Leadership.   2. Management.   3. Executive ability.
4. Strategic Planning   I. Title

HD57.7.F559   1999   98-39066
658.4'092—dc21   CIP

Printed in the United States of America
99 00 01 02 03 04 05 06 BVG 9 8 7 6 5 4 3 2 1

DEDICATION

To the leadership team
of CBInternational

I can't imagine working day by day
with a more gifted, committed, and yet humble
group of servant leaders.

You make leadership truly rewarding.

CONTENTS

FOREWORD

TAKE ONE GLANCE at this book and you quickly discover this is not simply another book on leadership. This is no old, worn-out dolly dressed up in new clothes. For one of those, just stop by a crowded airport newsstand and glance over the choice of books on leadership for today.

If you're like me, you've grown weary of the published cookie-cutter approaches on how to lead effectively. Somehow the church has aligned itself with Wall Street and traded its eternal values for matters better suited for leaders of microchip companies and ad agencies. I've gotten tired of all the hype surrounding church growth. And so has Hans Finzel. Instead he drills to the core, answering questions like, "What is the *real* biblical model of leadership?" "Does character matter?" "What qualities truly count for the Christian leader today?"

Refreshingly, with superb skill and an unusual knack for drawing you into his own experience, Finzel simply states that our only hope for finding clear direction in the soupy malaise of postmodern leadership theory is to refocus on the absolutely reliable compass of God's Word. It's about time someone said that.

So with the right compass in hand, the author steadily guides his readers on a satisfying journey toward rediscovering the timeless and rewarding disciplines of meditating on the Scriptures, prayer, and cultivating the inner spiritual life. To Finzel, integrity *does* matter. So he gently reminds us of the importance of pursuing such goals as character, creativity, and encouragement in leadership. All his discussions are carefully grounded in the Scriptures. And all his insights are seasoned with delightful real-life stories that not only convince, but refresh the weary soul like a tonic.

Highlighting such mammoth biblical leaders as Moses, Joseph, and David, this careful student of the Word emphasizes the often-missed truth that leaders are never perfect. Yet the best ones are authentic, and thus are usable by God. In other words effective leaders have feet of clay, but deep within are hearts of pure gold. The magnificent result is that the character studies in this book are full of fresh insights—insights that provide principles for effective leadership that you and I can implement and measure in any Christian setting.

You can't discern how to become an effective Christian leader merely by studying charts and analyzing demographic reports. True leadership is about understanding God, yourself, and those whom He has called you to lead. That takes time. And it takes prayer. And more time and more prayer. In the nucleus of such disciplines is a deep commitment to a life of studying and applying God's Word.

So locate your compass and prepare yourself for an unforgettable journey. You will soon be on your way to the fulfilling land of effective leadership. With Hans Finzel as your guide, I am convinced you will arrive there encouraged and wiser!

—CHARLES R. SWINDOLL
General Editor

ACKNOWLEDGMENTS

THIS PROJECT WAS A BIG JOB in the midst of a hectic life. A special thank you goes to my wife, Donna, a wonderful life companion for these twenty-three years, who helped make this manuscript come together. On top of the pressure of running the Finzel household with our two teenagers and ten-year-old twins, and covering the home front during all my travels, she gave many hours to editing and revising this manuscript. Her gifts in writing and insights into leadership have made a big difference, and for that I am very grateful. Thanks for spending all those hours in front of the computer, for your excellent feedback, for believing in me, and for always being there to make us successful as partners for life.

INTRODUCTION

LEADERSHIP IS DANGEROUS WORK. Just ask Captain Smith. On Sunday, April 14, 1912, a calm moonless night, the temperature was just about at the freezing mark. Inside, the passengers were enjoying a lovely dinner in the warm lively atmosphere of the newly christened *Titanic*.

Meanwhile in the wireless room Jack Phillips and Harold Bride were busy receiving ice warnings from other ships in the area. These messages were passed on to Captain Smith and the officers, who regarded them as normal warnings for this time of year and no threat to the *Titanic*. When the *Titanic* came in contact with Cape Race, Newfoundland, around 9:30 P.M., the wireless room became very busy sending passengers' routine messages to friends, relatives, and business contacts. During this time the most important ice warnings were ignored. The steamer *Mesaba* sent an urgent message, reporting that a large icefield lay in the direction in which the *Titanic* was headed.

Up in the crow's nest Frederick Fleet was staring into the darkness. Around 11:30 P.M., he noticed a black object immediately in their path. He urgently called the iceberg warning down to the officer in charge.

On the bridge First Officer Murdoch ordered "full speed astern" and "hard a starboard." Slowly the ship began to turn and it looked as if it would clear the ice. When they heard a strange scraping noise, Murdoch knew they had hit an iceberg, a seaman's worst nightmare. He then ordered the watertight doors shut.

Shortly after the collision Thomas Andrews, master builder of the ship, met with Captain Smith and gravely informed him that the *Titanic* was doomed. Over two hundred feet of the ship had been sliced open by the iceberg, and the first six watertight compartments were flooding.

Knowing his ship was sinking, Captain Smith ordered the evacuation of the *Titanic*. Their greatest problem was that the *Titanic* carried only enough lifeboats for about half the twenty-two hundred people on board. Meanwhile the wireless operators were sending distress calls indicating the *Titanic*'s position.

She went under at 2:20 A.M., less than three hours after striking the ice. Shortly after, all cries for help fell silent. All that was left of that greatest of passenger ships were partially filled lifeboats floating in a sea of blackness.

For Captain Smith, who went down with the ship, *his past leadership effectiveness was his greatest enemy*. He assumed he had mastered the art of leadership and grew cavalier at a time when he needed to be more careful than ever. The man everyone thought was the model captain made many fatal mistakes that night, and his errors cost the lives of 1,517 people. The ship itself (like the organizations we are asked to lead) was as sound as could be imagined. But the captain took that ship and sank it with his careless leadership choices.

The *Titanic* sank because its highly experienced captain made one flawed decision after another:

- He was blinded by his natural instincts.
- He undercalculated his enemies, the icebergs.
- He overcalculated his strengths, the strength of the ship.
- He took too many risks with his crew and his ship.
- He became reckless, pushing the ship too hard.
- His pride got in the way of effective leadership.
- He took ill-advised counsel from the ship owner to charge ahead.
- He left subordinates in command at a dangerous time.
- He was overconfident of the latest technology.

- He relied too much on past experience.
- He did not know his ship as well as he thought he did.
- He ignored repeated warnings of impending danger.
- He ignored the natural realities of the environment of that sea.

Who is to blame for the sinking of the *Titanic*? Captain Smith was surely to blame, but there were others at fault as well. The designer/builder and shipline owner, both also on the boat that night, were reckless and prideful about the abilities of their ship. They too were part of the doomed leadership team. Together these three leaders were responsible for one of the greatest preventable maritime tragedies.

Leadership is indeed filled with risk. The organizations we lead are much like the great oceanliners or smaller vessels that sail the seas of life. We the leaders are captains who are given the responsibility of taking care of the people in the boat with us. It is a great and high calling but not without its pitfalls. We have the awesome opportunity to do great good for the kingdom of God, but we face the real possibility of seriously hurting not only our lives but those of our followers as well.

History is filled with examples of good and bad leaders. We can look to the positive list of leaders as diverse as Thomas Edison, Abraham Lincoln, Amy Carmichael, John Rockefeller, Thomas Watson, Leonardo da Vinci, Mother Teresa, and Princess Diana. Some provided excellent leadership in government, others in the world of business, charity, industry, arts, and sciences. History is also filled with leaders who have done irreparable damage, such as Joseph Stalin, Adolf Hitler, and Benito Mussolini. They were gifted leaders who used their authority to do great harm. Whether the leaders did good or ill, their role was one of influence.

The word *influence* is the best one-word definition of leadership. After careful study on the subject, purposeful observation of leaders, and courses I've taken and taught, I always come back to that one simple definition which sums it all up: *influence.*

> *Leaders are people who influence others to think, feel, or act in certain ways.*

Whether for good or ill, leaders take followers places through the power of their influence.

Leadership is much tougher today than it was in some other eras. Some people idolize the World War II league of leaders who came back from winning the war. They applied their guts and courage, attempted great things, and were successful. But our world flatly rejects the authoritarian style those leaders employed. Most churches no longer accept top-down autocratic pastors. Today's organizational cultures have made authoritarianism obsolete.

Lou Holtz recently retired as head football coach for Notre Dame University after taking them to more than one hundred wins in his eleven-year tenure. He says the biggest problem in trying to lead today is that everyone is talking about *rights* and *privileges*, whereas twenty-five years ago people talked about *obligations* and *responsibilities*. Yet he adjusted his coaching style to deal successfully with the new mind-set and thus to lead his team to one victory after another. I applaud flexible older leaders who, like Lou Holtz, have seen the trends of change in leadership style and have made the switch. His observation contrasts builder values and boomer/buster values. When my turn comes to be one of the "next-to-be-retired" generation of leaders, I hope I will have Holtz's type of flexibility and learning ability. I'll need that as I continue to deal with the normal cultural changes that will confront me and other leaders of my generation in our ever-changing world.

I am enthusiastic about the new generation of leaders. In today's churches we find excellent leadership representing all the generations. Men and women of great integrity are giving effective leadership in all walks of life and in all disciplines. But many churches and organizations are hungering to find new leaders to fill their pulpits and leadership positions. At times there seems to be a shortage of qualified leaders.

Just what does it take to be effective in leadership today? In this book we will discuss principles of effective leadership, taking those principles from Scripture, our frame of reference. Like secular history, the Scriptures are filled with models of good and bad leadership. From great men like Abraham, Moses, David, Peter, and Paul to the wicked kings of Israel and traitors like Herod and Judas, we find leaders of all kinds. If the Bible were merely a book of fairy tales, I doubt the failures of leaders would have been included. But we find brutal reality in the Scriptures, in which some leaders are called friends of God and other leaders murdered their own sons and daughters. You will see a crucial difference in the lives of the biblical leaders cited in this book. The influence of these biblical men and women as leaders is obvious; their impact as leaders increased as they were empowered by God in their leadership.

Someone has said that leadership, like cream, rises to the top. Often leadership is not something a person volunteers for. It is something a person is chosen for by others as he or she rises through the ranks. So why is someone chosen to lead? What are the characteristics, skills, abilities, and personality that cause some people to be selected for leadership?

As stated already, leadership is risky, even dangerous. This is because you as a leader have the incredible opportunity to do good and to encourage large numbers of people to accomplish great things for God. A leader's influence can be used to build and lead organizations and movements that can help change the world. But as a leader, you can cause great destruction. We've all seen leaders who have taken missteps that have allowed their egos to grow too large, and those who got themselves into deep trouble ethically and morally, causing great devastation to their followers. These leaders placed a dark smudge on the reputation of the church of our Lord Jesus Christ.

In light of this we need to be careful when we embark on the leadership journey. It is a sobering responsibility with the potential for great good but also the potential for causing others to stumble. James warned, "Not many of you should presume to be teachers, my brothers, because you know that we who teach will be judged more strictly" (James 3:1).

The Lord Jesus Himself shared the delights and demands of leadership. He said, "Who then is the faithful and wise manager, whom the master puts in charge of his servants to give them their food allowance at the proper time? It will be good for that servant whom the master finds doing so when he returns. I tell you the truth, he will put him in charge of all his possessions. . . . From everyone who has been given much, much will be demanded; and from the *one who has been entrusted with much*, much more will be asked" (Luke 12:42–44, 48, italics added).

What's so great about leadership? Leadership is about influencing people for good. It is about accomplishing more through others than we could ever do on our own. People are what it is all about, and leadership is taking groups of people to exciting places they would not attempt on their own. Though at times I find myself totally inadequate for my job, I am thankful for the opportunity that my responsibilities give me to make an impact in the world. God gives increased ability when we need it. The empowered leader is intimately aware of his need to depend on the Lord constantly.

Regardless of how you became a leader and how far along you are on the journey, you can enjoy the expedition. God can use you to advance His purposes in your life and in the lives of those you lead. John Ruskin once said, "When a man is wrapped up in himself, he makes a pretty small package." Leadership is a self*less* journey that involves devoting yourself to a group of people to accomplish great things for the Lord that you could never do alone. And when leadership is carried out effectively, people make great things happen!

1

THE LEADER

Who Can Fill the Shoes?

"This is the same Moses whom they had rejected with
the words, 'Who made you ruler and judge?'" (Acts 7:35)

OF ALL THE THINGS I ENJOY in my typical day, one of my favorites takes place when I arrive home in the evening. Not that I don't love
my job; it's just that my children can make me feel greatly loved. The
harder the day I have had at the office, the more I enjoy their "ambush."

Our twins, Andrew and Cambria, are still young enough to be home
when I get home, to notice when I get home, and to jump with glee at the
sight of my coming through the kitchen door. We have this great ritual: I
come in from the garage, drop my briefcase, and my twins take turns
taking a running start across the room and zooming up into my arms.
They grab me around the neck and squeeze me so tight that all the stress
of the day just fades away.

After the hugfest has ended, I take off my shoes, grab the mail, and
settle down with a cup of coffee. Soon I hear the kids clomping across the
kitchen floor; they have managed to put their feet into my shoes. They
want to be like daddy. My youngest son even tells me, "Daddy, when I
grow up I am going to be the director of CBI!"

I wonder how much they really know about the cost of leadership.
Why would anyone want to grow up and become a leader? It may look
like fun on the outside, but little do they know the challenges. Being in
charge seems like the ideal place to be—but is it?

1

WHAT IT TAKES

What does it take to make it in today's leadership world? Though much has changed, a great deal about leadership is the same today as it has been throughout the centuries. Leaders need a compass now more than ever, and God has given us a most reliable one in His Word. The timeless truths we find in the Scriptures apply to today's complex world. There are valuable lessons leaping out at us from every one of the heroes and villains of old. Two such men are Saul and David.

Let's rewind our clocks of history a few thousand years to the early days of God's established nation of Israel. Having rejected God as King, the infant nation Israel made a poor leadership decision. Insisting on having a human king like the nations around them, they chose Saul. Appointing Saul as king over Israel brought serious consequences to this young nation. We could say it was in a leadership crisis. Saul presumed he could lead Israel according to his own inclinations, in clear disobedience to God. But he was sadly mistaken!

On one occasion Saul's disobedience involved taking the situation into his own hands, without waiting on God's prophet, Samuel. The fear of imminent attack by his enemy displayed Saul's lack of trust in God. God rebuked him through Samuel: " 'You acted foolishly,' Samuel said. 'You have not kept the command the LORD your God gave you; if you had, he would have established your kingdom over Israel for all time. But now your kingdom will not endure; the LORD has sought out a man after his own heart and appointed him leader of his people, because you have not kept the Lord's command' " (1 Sam. 13:13–14).

It was now time to pick the *right* man to do the job effectively—a successor to Saul. Of course God does not make mistakes, and in fact He had planned to appoint Saul as Israel's first leader. Among other things it showed the people of God what they would get for leadership when they stepped out ahead of Him. Here is a lesson for those involved today on search committees for new leadership: *Don't get ahead of God's leading as you seek His wisdom in making the right decision.* What you think you need and what He knows you need may differ completely.

I have seen many groups react in panic to the loss of their leader and hastily choose a successor who is not the right fit.

Take the time necessary to wait on God, do your homework, and select the right person carefully.

In the pressure cooker of organizational life this is one decision that must not be hurried. If you are the one applying for a position, don't be hasty in your decision; seek God's clear direction.

What was so special about David that God should choose him? He stood up to lions, bears, and Goliath not because his decision-making board of directors tapped him on the shoulder for leadership; rather, he was given strength to lead because God saw that *he had a heart for God.*

Being tapped on the shoulder for leading Israel was the last thing on David's mind. The first thing on his mind was his sheep. His pure simple faith in God enabled him to care for those sheep faithfully. That's about all we know about this young teenager, along with the fact that he played the harp, loved to sing, and was dutiful to his father. Yet, when Samuel asked Jesse to bring out his sons so that one of them could be selected to succeed Saul, it became apparent that God's decision-making process differs from man's. Samuel thought he knew God's pick, but he was wrong. The Lord said to Samuel, "Don't judge by his appearance or height, for I have rejected him. The LORD doesn't make decisions the way you do! People judge by outward appearance, but the LORD looks at a person's thoughts and intentions" (1 Sam. 16:7, NLT).

There is a certain irony in the fact that none of the older sons of Jesse measured up. To Samuel they seemed excellent candidates for God's leader. As soon as he saw Eliab, Jesse's oldest, Samuel thought, "Surely the Lord's anointed stands here before the LORD" (16:6). But God rejected all those admirable men. He was on the lookout for that certain special quality of heart essential for effective leadership. Jesse's other sons might have provided fair leadership, but David was God's choice.

Seeking to obey God in anointing a new king, Samuel was puzzled. "Are these all the sons you have?" (16:11) he asked. Jesse replied, "There is still the youngest, but he's out in the fields watching our sheep." God saw what man could not see. He knew David had what it takes to be a leader.

This story of David being chosen as king of Israel underscores principles related to aspiring for leadership, leadership selection criteria, and how God puts His hand on certain people for special leadership.

We'll explore David's story further, when we focus in chapters 2 and 3 on the *task* and the *character* of a leader.

DEFINING A "LEADER"

What does a leader look like? Stated another way, what does a person have to be and do to be considered an effective leader?

I shy away from mentioning present-day leaders whom I admire. No sooner do we put their names in print than they may crash and burn. The only safe examples are great leaders of the past. In that category I would place men and women like Martin Luther, Amy Carmichael, Adoniram Judson, Jim Elliott, Henrietta Mears, Charles Hadden Spurgeon, D. L. Moody, and Mother Teresa. Great secular leaders include Abraham Lincoln, Winston Churchill, Indira Gandhi, and Martin Luther King, Jr. (a leader in both secular and sacred arenas).

We can't help but think about other leaders who have affected us as we contemplate our own role in leadership. In my twenty years of ministry, I look back and think about those men and women I have most admired for their roles of leadership. What was it about them that inspired me? What is it about them that continues to challenge me to rise above my own limitations and attempt to *be* more and *do* more for the cause of Christ? I suggest seven qualities, which follow the acrostic of the word *Leaders*.

SEVEN LEADERSHIP QUALITIES

L —Long-term record of effectiveness. Leadership is not like squash that grows up rapidly and bears fruit within six months. Leadership is like the giant oak that takes years to develop and can withstand the greatest storm because of that slow building process. I have given up admiring people who have a short-term successful track record because it's the long haul that counts.

E —Egos surrendered to Christ. Unfortunately our Christian celebrity culture develops great personalities who can become overinfatuated with their own importance. Instead, I admire those people who are truly great but don't know it. Fortunately there are many of those around. Even if they realize how significant their influence is, their humble, gentle spirit is appreciated.

A —Approachable. This builds on the last point and has to do with the accessibility of a leader. I appreciate those men and women who are in leading roles and yet can be approached and treat everyone as important. This can sometimes place great pressure on leaders who have constant people demands; but I certainly try to make it my own practice to give attention and respect to anyone who approaches me.

D —Devotion to spouse and family. Many Christian leaders have become workaholics and at times sacrifice their marriages and children for the sake of "God's work." But God is not pleased with that approach; it is certainly not His design for leadership. If God has given a leader a spouse and children, then that leader is responsible to nurture those relationships with faithfulness. Respected leaders are those who have good marriages and have done their best to raise children who will follow with their own faith in the Lord.

E —Excellence in work. This means doing the best with what you have. Christians should aim for excellence in all they do. We appreciate those leaders who are obsessed with making their organizations excellent in every way. "Doing things right" is a culture that develops in organizations based on the pace the leader sets.

R —Reflection of Christlikeness in character. In the secular world some leaders have accomplished incredible feats—the Lee Iacoccas and Bill Gateses of the world. But in the body of Christ, my respect lies with those leaders who not only can do great things and have the ability to communicate effectively, but who also reflect the fruit of the Holy Spirit outlined in Galatians 5:22–23. Christ is our greatest example of effective leadership, and His character is the standard for our own leadership characteristics.

S —Sharing with others. Some leaders cut themselves off from others and are interested only in building their own empires. They have an exclusive attitude that works solely on building up their self-focused interests and their own organizations. The preferred kind of leader is the one who shares freely with other organizations, realizing that all believers are members of the body of Christ. This mentality reflects a simple maxim: It's amazing what we can get accomplished if we don't care who gets the credit.

Among the many leadership heroes in history, the top models are the characters of the Bible who were used by God because they fulfilled these seven qualities. In the following chapters I discuss five leaders in the Scriptures who embody the principles outlined in each of the coming chapters. The five characters are these:

- *Moses,* who became a great hero in extremely difficult circumstances and showed the potential of a reluctant leader.
- *David,* who shows what God looks for as He selects leaders to do His work.
- *Joseph,* who demonstrates the fruit of long-term faithfulness and maintaining a positive attitude based on faith in God.
- *Esther,* who exemplifies creativity and encouragement in a national crisis.
- *Paul,* who embodies the principles of durability in crises, who knew how to mentor a team, and who wrote about the rewards of sacrificial leadership.

One thing we see even in this list of biblical leaders is that not one of them was perfect. None of them maintained a Christlike attitude throughout every moment of their career. They all had bitter disappointments and none ever reached perfection. Why do we expect our leaders to be perfect? Why do we have such unrealistic expectations? If you are a leader, I know you appreciate it when those who follow you give you extra helpings of grace at every turn. We should be marked as a community of grace that expects great things from our leaders but gives generous grace when they fail. And conversely we who lead need to treat our followers with an equal helping of grace, allowing them room to fail and to develop as effective partners with us.

Some aspects of leadership selection have to do with *calling* and *motive,* with *fit* and *fulfillment.* Some leaders are reluctant to become leaders, others have doubts about their leadership abilities, and others have a heartfelt desire to be leaders for God.

ARE WE ALL RELUCTANT LEADERS?

I have observed a common trait of "reluctant leadership" during my twenty-year pilgrimage in leadership. I see it in myself and in just about every leader I talk to. From the early days of my experience—from laboring side by side with coworkers, to being in various levels of leadership, to finally landing in the corner office at headquarters as the person in charge—I have sensed a hesitation to move on to greater responsibility. Children may think being a leader solves all the problems of life, but adulthood brings the rude awakening that it's not that simple. With the privileges of leadership come many confinements.

Growing in leadership responsibilities is a two-sided coin. On one side there is a reluctance to take the next assignment. But on the other is a willingness and even excitement, tempered with a certain sense of nervousness, fear, and dread. The excitement of leadership is certainly there when you think about all the great things you hope to be able to accomplish. But the downside is just as real. I remembering crying out to God, "Are You sure You know what You're doing? Are You sure You have the right guy?" After all, the fewer your responsibilities in an organization, the less demanding is your schedule. The people at the helm are the ones who face serious decisions and are consumed with overwhelming issues. Recently a leader told me, "Before I finally accepted my new job, I turned it down three times, not because I did not know what I was getting into but because *I did know!*" Yes, God does place and use reluctant leaders.

When you're among the rank and file, you have to deal only with the problems and issues in your own corporate corner. Such a position certainly gives you a lot more discretionary time for your spouse, children, and hobbies! A person may feel he's a nobody in his tiny cubicle in the great corporate world in which he works, but maybe he should count his blessings. The buck stops nowhere near his desk!

Moses is one of the first great examples of this principle that God uses reluctant leaders. How did he feel when God made him go back from the desert to Egypt to lead the people out of bondage? Not very motivated, to say the least! He had no wish to attempt to lead a group of people who had clearly rejected him.

"This is the same Moses whom they had rejected with the words, *'Who made you ruler and judge?'* He was sent to be their ruler and deliverer by God himself, through the angel who appeared to him in the bush. He led them out of Egypt and did wonders and miraculous signs in Egypt, at the Red Sea and for forty years in the desert" (Acts 7:35–36, italics added).

Between verses 35 and 36 a significant event in Moses' life is purposefully omitted. Against Moses' objections, God had to drag Moses out of the desert and back to the people of Israel. Even though God appeared to him in a burning bush, Moses argued much with God before he finally accepted the leadership challenge: "But Moses said to God, 'Who am I, that I should go to Pharaoh and bring the Israelites out of Egypt?'" (Exod. 3:11).

God patiently answered that objection with a long list of the things He would do to ensure that the elders of Israel would listen to Moses. But Moses said again, "What if they do not believe me or listen to me and say, 'The LORD did not appear to you'?" (4:1).

We have to admire our Father in heaven for not giving up on Moses. After this argument God decided to offer many signs and proofs to legitimize his leadership. The Lord armed Moses with a convincing arsenal of proofs that he was to be God's spokesman. But Moses was not convinced. He argued that he had no speaking ability. "Moses said to the LORD, 'O Lord, I have never been eloquent, neither in the past nor since you have spoken to your servant. I am slow of speech and tongue'" (4:10).

Still not worn down by objections, God assured Moses, "I will help you speak and will teach you what to say" (4:12). Would it not make sense that by now reticent Moses would trust God and His promises of help? God was assuring Moses that He would take care of everything; but He was also saying that He needed a man to lead His people to freedom. A side lesson of this story is the truth that God really does rely on people to do His will on earth. He could have chosen angels or other means, but His method is always men and women, even if they are frail or reluctant.

Moses replied one more time to God: "O Lord, please send someone else to do it" (4:13). At that point God got angry and appointed Aaron as the spokesman of Moses. Every time I read this story I marvel at the grace the Father showed to Moses; I wonder again why it had to be Moses. The answer is that *God wanted him for who he was*, despite his reluctance. Moses did indeed turn out to be one of the great leaders of God's redemptive plan.

Recently I was speaking to a large gathering of the leaders who head up our ministries in different countries around the world. Currently our mission has people working in about sixty countries worldwide. We were addressing the issues of their pilgrimages to their positions of leadership. Almost without exception I found that these men and women were in the same boat I was in, reluctant to lead. Most of them had the Moses complex. They did not volunteer for or ask for leadership responsibilities. We asked them to consider accepting those responsibilities because of their spiritual gifts and experience. They were willing to give it a try, or in some cases they were elected to their leadership roles by their peers. Some of them were the only ones available or willing to work in that role. People come into leadership positions for various reasons. No matter how it happens, it seems that one day you wake up and there you are—the leader!

The higher you go in leadership responsibility, the less opportunity you have to volunteer for positions of influence. You tend to be selected either by your peers, a group of executives above you, or some sort of corporate body or search committee. A pastor may search for a church to lead, but the process is not really in his control.

> *One of the great traits search committees should look for is an openness and willingness to serve, a servant's heart.*

In fact I shy away from choosing people who are overly aggressive, maneuvering, and politicking for positions of leadership. The best leaders are those who are tapped from a pool of faithful and effective workers, and who are willing, if asked, to rise to the next level. Search committees have learned through the years that their best candidates will often be those people who are not themselves searching. Reluctant leaders are often the best leaders.

As we gathered with that group of leaders from around the world, it became apparent that they were all willing but reluctant to serve in leadership. Like the local church, ours is a not-for-profit organization. We can't provide extra financial incentives for higher positions of leadership. We met with these for a four-day workshop called a "Summit on Leadership Training." As we listened to their concerns, two requests were prominent: (a) "Tell us what a leader is supposed to look like," and (b) "Equip us to be that kind of leader."

Excellent! These responses were just what we, the trainers of the leaders, needed to hear. In fact, based on the input we received from these field personnel, we embarked on a process of defining the role of leadership in our organization and then developing a program that would equip them to move toward that profile. We knew that becoming an effective leader is a process; it takes years and is in many ways a continual work in progress. These reluctant leaders are now well on their way to being more effective in the ministries in which God has placed them.

A. W. Tozer commented on this common trait of reluctance. He observed that the best leaders have no desire to lead. Like calling draftees into an army, God chooses men and women who are willing to give it a go.

A true and safe leader is likely to be one who has no desire to lead, but is forced into a position of leadership by the inward pressure of the Holy Spirit and the press of the external situation. Such were Moses and David and the Old Testament prophets. I think there was hardly a great leader from Paul to the present day but that was drafted by the Holy Spirit for the task, and commissioned by the Lord of the Church to fill a position he had little heart for. I believe it might be accepted as a fairly reliable rule of thumb that the man who is ambitious to lead is disqualified as a leader. The true leader will have no desire to lord it over God's heritage, but will be humble, gentle, self-sacrificing and altogether as ready to follow as to lead, when the Spirit makes it clear that a wiser and more gifted man than himself has appeared.[1]

LEADERSHIP DOUBT

Some of you who read these pages may be struggling with another fundamental question: "Am I really a leader or not?" Rather than being reluctant, you may doubt whether you can do the job. Many leaders struggle with that question. One pastor wrote me, "The scary issue often comes up to me (almost never admitted, but given some time in every pastor's mind), 'What if I'm not really gifted to be a leader? Is that okay? How can I compensate? Do I need to turn in my ordination papers? Resign my position?'"

What we have here is a major misperception of what leadership is. My friend helped confirm how many leaders are thinking these kinds of thoughts—although we often don't feel safe in verbalizing them to our followers; after all, it could cost us our jobs! He added, "I think we are ending up forcing many pastors to deceive themselves into thinking they are leaders, playing the role, getting the training, reading the right books, and then losing the energy for ministry because deep down it is not their thing."

Maybe you feel like my friend. If so, read on! Help is on the way. When I read his words, I realized this discouraging reality: We have not done a good job in communicating what leadership really is. Some leaders imagine that what people want in their leader is a Norman Schwartzkopf type of powerful individual, in front of whom all enemies melt in submission. He is the one who can win the victory in any battle and who always knows the right call in any situation. Nothing ruffles his composure, and he commands everyone's respect. His skin is so thick that no amount of criticism breaks through to the inside.

God's leaders, however, don't need to be like "Stormin' Norman"! Remember that leadership is defined by the simple word *influence*. If you influence others in small ways or large, then you are involved in leadership. Someone who has opportunities to influence others is a leader.

Ted Engstrom makes a helpful distinction between a real view versus the perceived view of a leader. Using the example of the apostle Paul, who would tend to be the Schwartzkopf type, he observes, "For many Christian leaders, Paul's experience models and magnifies our own. Those of us who have been called to roles of leadership often say to ourselves, 'Why did God do all this for me? Why is He giving me these privileges of leadership?' We suspect not only that we really don't deserve God's grace, but also that we're actually not that good at what we're doing. Which man was the real Paul? Was he the one who led so confidently or the one who was deeply uncertain of his abilities? Most Christian leaders who have been tested in their leadership would probably answer, 'Both!' Christian leadership includes agony as well as ecstasy." [2]

IS IT WRONG TO WANT TO LEAD?

Some people are reluctant leaders. And for some who find themselves in positions of leadership, there are genuine feelings of doubt. But what about the others, those who really do aspire to positions of influence? Is it wrong to want to be a leader? Should you feel guilty if you enjoy it? Is it unspiritual to aspire to reach a certain level or position of influence? According to Paul, being a leader is a noble aspiration. "Here is a trustworthy saying: If anyone sets his heart on being an overseer, he desires a noble task" (1 Tim. 3:1). To want to be a leader for God is an honorable ambition! There's nothing wrong with wanting to be a leader, and there's nothing wrong with wanting to be an effective leader.

But related to the desire for leadership is the question of motive. *Why* do we want to be leaders in God's church? Why do we want to be in positions of influence? Is it for our egos, for the prestige that the positions bring with them? Is it to accomplish heroic deeds? Or is it to have the opportunity to exercise the spiritual gifts God has given us and to accomplish great things for Him? Every leader wrestles with this question of motive. We need to remember that immediately after Paul told Timothy it is okay for a believer to set his heart on being a leader, he listed high standards and qualifications: "Now the overseer must be above reproach, the husband of but one wife, temperate, self-controlled, respectable, hospitable, able to teach, not given to drunkenness, not violent but gentle, not quarrelsome, not a lover of money. He must manage his own family well and see that his children obey him with proper respect. . . . He must not be a recent convert, or he may become conceited and fall under the same judgment as the devil. He must also have a good reputation with outsiders, so that he will not fall into disgrace and into the devil's trap" (3:2–4; 6–7).

Impossible standards? Can anyone fit that bill? "Who is worthy?" you might be asking. If we did not have real-life examples from the Bible, we might never try to fit the bill. But there is good news for us all. We'll see from the lives of God's servant leaders in Scripture that He uses imperfect people to accomplish His will on earth. We serve as leaders with a God of high standards, but at the same time He is a God of infinite grace and mercy.

"A leader is someone whose actions have the most profound consequences on other people's lives, for better or for worse, sometimes forever
and ever."[3] The call to leadership is one of life's most challenging and
rewarding pursuits. It is rewarding from an eternal perspective. We began
this chapter with the question, Who can fill the shoes? The answer is simple
but not easy: *anyone who is willing to be used to influence a group of people
to accomplish grand objectives.*

As James Kouzes and Barry Posner stated, "Leaders are pioneers.
People who take the lead are the foot soldiers in the campaigns for
change. . . . The unique reason for having leaders—their differentiating function—is to move us forward. Leaders get us going someplace."[4]

2

THE TASK

A Leader's Work

"And David *shepherded* them with integrity of heart; with skillful hands he *led* them." (Ps. 78:72, italics added)

WARREN WILKE, an acquaintance of President Franklin D. Roosevelt, often spent time in the Oval Office. This man was unusual because apparently he was an alcoholic, often offended people, and didn't seem to contribute anything to discussions. Frankly, people wondered why Wilke hung around the Oval Office.

One day a reporter asked President Roosevelt why he kept this person around. Roosevelt responded by saying that if the reporter were president of the United States, he would cherish the opportunity to have at least one person come into the Oval Office who didn't want anything from him! He would be grateful for one person who simply wanted to sit in his presence and be his friend.

I've never met a leader who didn't feel trapped at times. Leadership can be a wonderful thing, but there are days and weeks when "trapped" is the best way to describe the experience. Many leaders then start searching want ads and brush up their resumés. The prophet Elijah shows us the principle that *the bigger the victory, the larger the next day's letdown may be.* Following one of his greatest victories, seeing the defeat of the prophets of Baal, Elijah hit one of his lowest points and ran for his life, hiding from Jezebel!

We should admit it: At times we in professional ministry look beyond

Christian want ads to other lines of work to get out of the pressure cooker altogether. "These guys who punch the clock and leave their troubles at the office have it made," we begin to rationalize. More often than we may choose to admit, we dream about what it would be like to be in totally different shoes. The grass in other pastures starts looking a lot greener.

How do men and women who seem to have their act together do it? We see highly successful leaders and we say, "And then there is me." It seems that leadership today involves more pressure than it ever has, and at times we wish we could go back to the bottom of the organizational chart or at least find some way to get rid of the criticism and pressure.

Leadership can be immensely rewarding. We see highly effective leaders influencing others for good and accomplishing great things. We wonder how we, too, can do that.

> *Leadership lies more in balancing the right things than in having the right gifts and personality.*

Even for those who may feel ready to bail out, learning and employing those right skills can put them back on solid footing. Many people in the Bible who made a profound difference as leaders can encourage us to keep trying. However weak they were, or timid, shy, or retiring, God chose to use them and they were willing and available to be used by Him.

THE REAL BALANCING ACT

The part of Jonathan Swift's fairy tale *Gulliver's Travels* I like most is when Gulliver is captured by tiny six-inch people and lies strapped to the ground with dozens of cords holding him down. The Lilliputians are climbing here and there on the giant, even standing on his stomach and forehead, having a great time with their prized catch. The ones standing on his nose are particularly triumphant, basking in their victory as the giant has been tamed.

As a leader, how many times have you felt trapped like Gulliver, tied down by lots of little people with hundreds of tiny ropes that have left you immobilized?

Gulliver groans as he twists and turns, trying to free himself from his captors and their ropes. For some reason this image has always been one of the most vivid descriptions of my own experience of leadership. Contrary to what most followers think, being a leader does not give you the freedom to come and go as you please. Quite the opposite. Leaders are tied to a multitude of people, responsibilities, processes, and systems. You have fewer choices rather than more.

- For a busy pastor, there are counseling, preaching, and the numerous needs and problems of church members.
- For the overworked (and underpaid) church staff member, there are demands from all sides for a piece of his or her time.
- For the busy manager, there are never enough hours in the day, especially since the latest downsizing has upsized his job!
- For the stressed-out executive, there are the demands of the board, the bottom line, travel, and decisions to be made.

Leadership is influence. Leadership is too much to do and not enough time.

Leadership is everyone wanting a piece of your time. Leadership is unrealistic expectations. Leadership is pressure from followers that never lets up. Leadership is a balancing act.

Leadership also has to do with being misunderstood. I am not saying that we are the "big shot" Gulliver-like leaders and that the followers are just insignificant little people. No; we are the servant leaders, and the followers are the key to the success of our enterprise. Leadership involves empowerment and "the equipping of the saints for the work of ministry" (Eph. 4:12, NKJV). Leadership is indirect ministry through the effectiveness of others.

In *Gulliver's Travels* the little people misunderstood Gulliver. He had no intention of harming them, but they didn't realize it. Another great pain of leadership is being misunderstood by the rank and file. Though we intend them to flourish, they at times think we are using them. And at times the very people we are trying to help rise up against us in rebellion.

How can we lead strongly and yet empower our followers to be strong in their own ministries? There is the rub, the balancing act. Since leadership is preparing others to do the work of this ministry, how can we help them without ending up like Gulliver? How do we lead them without letting them tie us down so much that we become trapped and stifled in our own leadership gifts?

THE HEART OF A LEADER

Who better illustrates this fine balancing act than David, a man after God's own heart? King David had the unusual ability to be both a skillful leader and to have a pure heart. Something about David's heart captivated the Lord and thrust him into tremendous leadership responsibilities.

This second chapter focuses on a leader's *work*. What is the job of leadership and what are its essential components? Chapter 3 deals more in depth with the critical issue of *character*. What is the kind of person God uses in long-term effective leadership? The *task* and the *person* are two of the most crucial elements for leading effectively.

David was effective in leadership because he was a man who balanced these two components. He illustrates well both strength of character and skill in work. Psalm 78 is a depressing litany strewn with the failure of God's people. But it does not end on the bad news. In the midst of bad news God raised up leaders to turn the situation around. Repeatedly God raised up leaders to speak to His people to guide and lead them, and they failed. "He decreed statutes for Jacob and established the law in Israel, which he commanded our forefathers to teach their children, so the next generation would know them, even the children yet to be born, and they in turn would tell their children. Then they would put their trust in God and would not forget his deeds but would keep his commands. They would not be like their forefathers—a stubborn and rebellious generation, whose hearts were not loyal to God, whose spirits were not faithful to him" (Ps. 78:5–8).

This psalm begins with the hope that future generations would not repeat the sins of the past. But that hope was dashed. "But they continued to sin against him, rebelling in the desert against the Most High" (78:17).

Then God blessed them with manna from heaven and gave them all the provisions they needed for their desert journey. But in the midst of all this, were they coming around? Not at all. "In spite of all this, they kept on sinning; in spite of his wonders, they did not believe" (78:32).

This is a sad, depressing story of a people who were disobedient and arrogant before God. Psalm 78 continues with more of the same. But just when you're about to close the book and give up on God's people, along comes a leader who changes the day! Tucked away in the last three verses is hope! And that hope is in a man, a young shepherd boy who would become one of the great leaders of biblical history. "He chose David his servant and took him from the sheep pens; from tending the sheep he brought him to be the shepherd of his people Jacob, of Israel his inheritance. And David *shepherded* them with integrity of heart; with skillful hands he *led* them" (78:70–72, italics added).

David had the balance between the heart for the task and the skill to do the task. As mentioned in chapter 1, in God's choosing David to lead the nation He sent Samuel to Jesse's family to anoint one of his sons as the future king. Jesse brought out son after son—seven in all—and each time father and son were disappointed when Samuel said the lad was not God's choice.

The very son Jesse thought was least qualified was the very one God had in mind. The Lord's thoughts are rarely our thoughts, and His ways usually differ from ours (Isa. 55:8–9). So Jesse had David brought in. "He was ruddy, with a fine appearance and handsome features" (1 Sam. 16:12). Later one of Saul's servants gave additional information about David's experience and qualifications: "I have seen a son of Jesse of Bethlehem who knows how to play the harp. He is a brave man and a warrior. He speaks well and is a fine-looking man. And the LORD is with him" (16:18).

When David appeared before Samuel, the Lord told the prophet, "Rise and anoint him; he is the one" (16:12).

Again we see how those who do not seek for leadership are often the best qualified to lead. Probably all seven of David's brothers wanted to be tapped on the shoulder. One by one, their hearts were filled with excitement when each of them anticipated the possibility that *he* would be the one. No doubt they were bitterly disappointed that not one of them had been selected. When David was brought in and chosen, they must have been livid that their little brother was *the* one. Everyone who has raised children knows the dynamics of sibling rivalry.

The explanation of why God chose David is so clear. Years ago, as a young Christian in my twenties, I memorized this verse. Meditating on it I found a richness of teaching about God's ways of selecting leadership. "Do not consider his appearance or his height, for I have rejected him. The LORD does not look at the things man looks at. Man looks at the outward appearance, but the LORD looks at the heart" (16:7). In the New Living Translation, the last clause in this verse reads, "but the LORD looks at a person's thoughts and intentions."

So God chose David, but he did not begin his leadership career until years later. David had what it took to do the task, but he had to wait to begin. In fact his patience in those early years is one of the great attributes for which we so admire David.

Waiting is a significant issue in leadership. Do you want to be a leader? Impatience is not a virtue. Be prepared to do a lot of waiting. Even when David knew he had been set aside by God to be king, he was very patient and willingly served in subservient roles in Saul's court. Leadership is like that. So much of leadership has to do with waiting for the right opportunity in God's perfect timing. Many of David's most powerful and encouraging psalms were written during this period of waiting on God's timing.

God painstakingly prepared David to be the right person, so that when the right moment came he had what it took to be the best king Israel ever had. This also was Daniel's experience. He, too, had years of waiting. Later in his life, after intervening years of obscurity following his service to Nebuchadnezzar, God needed his special gifts to interpret Belshazzar's dreams on the very last night of the Babylonian Empire (Dan. 5). Joseph, too, had a time of waiting. As a boy he knew his brothers and clansmen would one day serve him. But little did he know then all he would have to undergo to be made ready for that role of leadership.

So why did God choose David? Because of his *heart* and also because of his *skills*. One of the great Bible verses on leadership is Psalm 78:72, which we mentioned earlier. "And David shepherded them with integrity of heart; with skillful hands he led them." Acts 13:22 confirms that David's abilities had much to do with his selection: "After removing Saul, he made David their king. He testified concerning him: 'I have found David son of Jesse a man after my own heart; *he will do everything I want him to do*'" (italics added).

The remainder of this chapter discusses the "skillful hands" issue, the basic *work* of the leader. Then chapter 3, "The Person," discusses the matter of *character*, "integrity of heart."

When David died after his forty-year reign, one of the greatest eras in the history of Israel came to a close. G. Frederick Owen summarizes the essence of David's life, even against the backdrop of his character flaws. "David satisfied the people throughout Israel, and quieted the Philistines for all time to come, then in the midst of peace and plenty wrote many psalms of praise to Jehovah. The elderly king gathered vast stores of stone and iron, brass and cedar for the erection of the temple of God. He gave his parting charge, and closed the most successful royal career recorded in the annals of history."[1]

STAYING AT CENTER

What leader could ever say with honesty that he has nothing to do? Ask any leader what he does with his time, and no matter the size of the group he's responsible for, he will probably sigh and say, "You name it, I do it." One of the greatest challenges in leading skillfully is to focus on the work of the leader without being constantly pulled down into the minutiae of "follower work." Easy to say, but not easy to do.

My four children get tired of my favorite sayings, sayings that summarize life's essentials I feel they need to know. They roll their eyes and think, "There he goes again!" One of my top favorites is, "Life is messy." Well, leadership is "messy" in a sense; the job is never fully under your control. On any given morning when you walk into your office, you have no idea what might hit you broadside and ruin the great plans you had for that day:

- A financial crisis
- A moral crisis
- A morale crisis
- A wounded employee
- An angry employee or church member
- A project gone haywire
- Employees or members fighting with one another
- An unexpected resignation

- A nasty rumor
- A personal criticism

The list could go on. So what is a leader to do? Even when we face those "messy" times, a strong leader must always go back to the center. To focus on the task with skillful action as David did, we must strive each day to keep from being "lost in the trees." We must not allow unplanned issues to rule us. David was a mighty warrior, a skilled political leader, a king, a musician, and a poet. He was skillful in all he did as a leader, yet we don't really know his exact "how-to" list of what kept him at center.

I have developed my own list of leadership priorities that I call the "center" of a leader's work. These eight are key functions of a leader's work—tasks that compose whatever a leader should be responsible for. These elements are essential for pastors, other local-church leaders, and leaders of Christian and secular organizations.

The Eight Key Functions of the Leader

1. Cultivating the vision
2. Creating a clear organization
3. Choosing the right team
4. Changing the culture
5. Coaching the team
6. Caring for the troops
7. Curing the problems
8. Checking on progress

CULTIVATING THE VISION

Are you surprised that I did not title this first step of leadership something like "Creating the Vision" or "Discerning the Direction"? I purposefully use the word *cultivating* because my view puts a leader in the role of gathering the vision that resides in the leadership team.

> *The leader is the harvester or cultivator of the vision that in a sense is embodied in the lives of all the major stakeholders of the organization.*

That corporate vision, in conjunction with a prayerful seeking of God's direction for the group, is the best source of vision. Certainly when David began his reign as king, he had no idea where God would take him. He followed, he listened, and he learned.

A church's stakeholders are the pastor, the pastoral staff, the board of deacons and/or elders, and the congregation. Some church structures, with an elder-rule approach, allow the leaders to make decisions affecting the congregation, whereas other churches rely on the democracy of membership vote. In either case the leaders should cultivate the vision through careful dialogue with the stakeholders. (Chapter 6, "Vision," discusses this subject at greater length.)

An important thing to remember about vision is that the more the stakeholders have bought into the process of determining it, the more they will support that vision and be enthusiastic in helping the organization accomplish that vision. Thus a leader's role is to help major constituents cultivate and articulate that vision.

CREATING A CLEAR ORGANIZATION

Organizations are continually in the process of changing. One of the leader's tasks is to work constantly at adjusting the internal structures that organize the people and their departments.

Organizing is the work we do to put people and tasks together in a structure that works.

Organizing involves such things as creating organizational structures, delegating responsibilities, developing lines of authority, and devising job descriptions.

How a ministry or company is organized is not high on my list of priorities for effectiveness. Sometimes I think organizations could change their organizational charts without making a lot of difference. Some newly appointed leaders begin immediately to effect major restructuring and reorganizing, but the results are often disappointing.

Much more important issues of culture, integrity, values, and vision make or break an organization. However, the leader's task is to work constantly at trying to make the organization flow logically and efficiently—in a manner that will best use available resources and help people understand lines of responsibility and authority. It is frustrating to work in situations where lines of authority and responsibility are not clearly delineated. Everyone should know to whom they are to report and what their basic job responsibilities are. When everyone is in charge, no one is in charge. It is the leader's job to organize the work in such a way that the group accomplishes God's plans for it.

CHOOSING THE RIGHT TEAM

If you surround yourself with the right people, you will succeed. The people around you will determine your level of success, so choose them well! Teams of people working together demonstrate how the body of Christ works in the church. Gifts each person brings to the team strengthen the whole. I enjoy seeing how God has given everyone on the leadership team with which I work different strengths to contribute to the fabric of our work as a whole. If we work in unison, we are putting the power of God's gifts to work in our midst.

One of the most important jobs you'll ever do as a leader is to choose the right people around you. The higher up those people are, the more important your task is of choosing them well. Ron Smith, a pastor in Florida, writes about the three Cs he always follows when he's hiring new staff.

I have what I call my three "Cs"—Commitment, Character and Competence. I think they are important in that order.

Commitment. First, when I seek to hire somebody on my staff or to choose someone to lead an area of ministry, I am most concerned about their commitment to Jesus Christ. I cannot convert anyone—that is the work of the Holy Spirit. I have seen too many of my friends make serious mistakes in hiring non-believers who were good people, but who did not share a heart for the ministry.

Character. If a person does not have strong character, then you have to re-parent them. A large part of ministry involves parenting or mentoring. A person on your team without the necessary *character* qualities takes years to re-parent. They are a drain on your team rather than an asset. If a person's parents did not instill in them the strong character traits of integrity, loyalty, tenacity, honesty, etc., then generally speaking you will spend years trying to do what the parents did not do. Who has that kind of time?

Competence. Certainly a person has to have basic skills. But all in all, I can send somebody to a seminar, send them to school, give them a book or a tape to listen to and help them develop their skills and competency in an area. I certainly want those serving with me to have good skills, but I find competency is often the easiest factor to develop in an individual.[2]

CHANGING THE CULTURE

Whether you like it or not, if you are anywhere near the top level of leadership in your organization, you are the keeper and developer of the culture of that organization. What is organizational "culture"? And what does it have to do with leadership? To many Christians working within traditional organizations, this is a new concept with little meaning.

The term *culture* was for many years reserved for the descriptive domain of the anthropologist and sociologist. But today it is a buzzword in management circles. Anyone who has an interest in leadership or management will encounter the concept of "corporate culture." Increasingly it is being recognized as one of the fundamental building blocks of effective leadership.

The culture of your organization can help determine whether your goals are reached. Culture is as powerful a force in an organization as it is in a foreign country. At times people get so devoted to their company they have an almost religious allegiance to its culture.

The term *culture* means different things to different people. The dilemma of defining the word *culture* is highlighted by William B. Renner, of the Aluminum Company of America. "Culture is different things to different people. For some, it's family or religion. It's opera or Shakespeare, a few clay pots at a Roman dig. Every textbook offers a definition, but I like a simple one: culture is the shared values and behavior that knit a community together. It's the rules of the game; the unseen meaning between the lines in the rulebook that assures unity. All organizations have a culture of their own."[3]

Learn how to analyze the values and the "rulebook" of the people you are asked to lead. *It is imperative that you uncover and come to grips with the unwritten but key values and norms of the culture of your organization.* This will help you immensely in bringing about change properly and in building allies. (In chapter 7 we will address how to manage change within an organization.)

COACHING THE TEAM

As we already noted, a leader is only as good as the team that surrounds him or her. This principle has become painfully obvious to everyone who has looked at leadership issues seriously over the past twenty years. Therefore place high priority on guiding and empowering your leadership team! Johnny Miller, president of Columbia International University, Columbia, South Carolina, wrote me about the changing leadership paradigms for the future. I could not agree more with his sentiment that we need to move from the model of the "out-front" visionary leader to the concept of the leader as a team builder. "I think the model of a leader as one person out in front of the pack is bound to change—must change. And it is in the realm of ministry that it is probably least likely to change. . . . I suggest that leaders are primarily team-builders and that in my role of leadership I find of greatest value [the acquiring of] people better than myself and freeing them to be heroes in our organization."[4]

When I speak of a leadership team, I refer to that group that works closest to the pastor or chief executive officer in leading the organization. This group may be the pastoral staff, the vice presidents, the elders, the cabinet, the executive committee, or whatever you call your close confidants. These are the men and women who constitute your leadership unit. Each person has strengths and weaknesses that together complement the whole and create a healthy synergy that makes leadership work. Building our teams and working with them is essential to our staying in the center of leadership. If you are a pastor, your staff and elders are your first concern. If you are a manager or chief executive officer in a ministry or business, your chief staff members are your "flock."

CARING FOR THE TROOPS

The old paradigm of leadership was based on the tough military model of a hardened command-and-control general. This model of leadership projected the image that softness was weakness. However, in recent years that model is changing. Books like *Love and Profit: The Art of Caring Leadership,* by James Autrey,[5] show how important it is that leaders care for their followers in the spirit of the apostle Paul, who nurtured his flock like a mother nurses her young. (I'll have more to say about caring for your people in chapter 4, "Encouragement," and chapter 8, "Your Leadership Team.")

Caring for the people who work for you involves providing the best possible resources and environment for every individual in your organization. Everything from salary and benefits to working conditions, facilities, equipment, and the building itself should be considered "tools of the trade."

You will be more successful as a whole as you care for each of the individual parts of your organization.

We don't want to treat our followers like children, but there are parallels to a parent and his child. As Donna and I are raising our four children, we are constantly thinking, "How can we create the kind of environment in which our children will grow up to be most succesful?" We want our children to have a safe, warm home, nourishing food, and clothing that will protect them and give them security to flourish as unique individuals within our family unit. When it comes to doing their schoolwork, we want them to have a good place to work with proper equipment and a home computer. With a computer, they have access to a wide variety of learning tools, so they can do the best job possible with their assignments. When it comes to sports, sometimes we've made the commitment to buy them the right kind of shoes, clothing, and other equipment so they can do their best in that endeavor. We recently purchased a piano so our children can enjoy and benefit from learning a musical instrument. These external things help our children to be stronger internally. It is part of the process of loving and caring for them and is an investment in their development. A leader has much of the same type of responsibility for his or her followers.

In the annual review I give to each of the individuals who reports to me, I ask them, "What can I or we as an organization provide for you that will help you be more effective next year?" I really want them to tell me what they need. As part of an exit interview, when a person leaves your organization or church, you might ask the question, "Why did you leave, and what would have changed things to keep you from leaving?" Some of the most profound insights I have learned to help make our organization a better place to work have been gleaned from exit interviews when people no longer feel their jobs are at stake when they tell me the truth.

CURING THE PROBLEMS

Some days I feel my only value to the people who walk into my office is to be their problem-solver. I certainly don't have to worry about not being wanted!

Some leaders like to be in the loop on every single problem that is solved, but I have the opposite philosophy of trying to push delegation downstream as far as possible. My motto is, "Blessed are the control freaks, for they shall inhibit the earth."

I want to create followers who are their own problem-solvers. That's part of effective delegation. However, problems keep percolating up the chain of command for a lot of reasons, including fear of failure, fear of taking responsibility, and fear of consequences. Many times some people feel nervous about being the ones ultimately responsible for a particular decision. The only way they can find comfort is to push that decision upstream, which often means they end up on the desk of the leader. That's the meaning of the saying, "The buck stops here."

Like salmon swimming upstream, many problems seem to have an uncanny ability to work their way up to my office. Although the leader's job *is* to solve many of those problems, *part of the problem-solving process should be to try to coach those people who bring problems to you to solve them on their own.* So I always ask the person who is bringing me a problem to tell me what he thinks the solution is. Ninety percent of the time I tell him to go with his own instincts. This way I try to wean them away from having to come to me with each situation. Hopefully they will leave my office saying to themselves, "Well, maybe next time I won't take that problem to him since he seems to think I would have made the right decision anyway."

Don't get the idea that you as a leader do not have to make many hard decisions. You do. But there is also the task of developing the leaders around you by allowing them maximum authority to make big decisions as well. *You have to make it clear to people exactly how much freedom and leeway they have to make their own decisions.* If you don't give people freedom to make decisions, they will keep coming back to you to make the decisions for them. Or if you jump down their throats for making poor decisions, then you can be sure they will keep coming back to you for *you* to make the decisions; they will want to avoid the pain of being criticized again.

CHECKING ON PROGRESS

I have great faith in people. I probably trust people too much; nine times out of ten I am overly optimistic about their productivity potential. However, I've also found that the reality of human nature is that people do what you inspect more than what you expect. So you have to build in some means of checking on the progress of the work.

Part of any working day in my life is given over to tracking and checking the progress of numerous projects that have been delegated throughout the organization. I'm not talking here about looking over shoulders, but about monitoring the progress of any given program. Most people need reminders, and I find that as a leader I am the ultimate "reminderer" in the organization. The people whom I most enjoy working with are those who are self-starters: self-disciplined individuals who bring me the results of their projects before I ever have a chance to check on their progress. After a while you learn whom you need to remind and whom you can count on to follow through without reminders.

I appreciate people in my organization keeping me informed of their progress without my having to ask. They are ideal followers. In fact, by taking initiative and leading in their own areas of responsibility they are showing great leadership potential.

The people who are discouraging to most leaders are those who have done nothing since the leader last checked on them. Then when the leader checks on their progress, they produce a spurt of activity because they are embarrassed with the checkup. But that spurt of activity will run out of steam until the next time their progress is checked. That kind of person— we all have them—is not self-motivated and self-directed and shows little leadership potential.

Leaders know the buck stops with them. I know my board holds me responsible for what I and my team accomplish as a group. A deacon and/ or elder board or an entire congregation judges its pastor for what is accomplished. So we must be fruit inspectors. Peter Drucker wrote about the unpopularity of leadership because of needing to get results. "An effective leader is not someone who is loved or admired. He or she is someone whose followers do the right things. Popularity is not leadership. Results are. Leaders are highly visible. They, therefore, set examples. Leadership is not rank, privilege, titles, or money. It is responsibility." [6]

In many ways it is impossible to summarize a leader's work in one chapter or even in one book. A leader's responsibilities seem endless at times. A friend of mine put it well as he was expressing frustration about his role as pastor: "I feel like a stray dog at a whistler's convention." There never seems to be an end to the demands people make on your time and energy.

One thing we know about David is that as a man of focus he accomplished much for God. Our world today seems a lot more complex than the world in which he lived. Yet he certainly had just as many distractions and problems as we do. A friend of mine in Hong Kong sent me a list of what he calls the "Seven Cs to Success in Leadership." Touching on some of the things we've mentioned already, it gives a practical point of view of a leader's task.

1. *Clarity.* Eighty percent of success comes from being clear on who you are, what you believe in, and what you want.
2. *Competence.* You can't climb to the next rung on the ladder until you are excellent at what you do now.
3. *Constraints.* Eighty percent of all obstacles to success come from within. Find out what is constraining you or your company and deal with it.
4. *Concentration.* The ability to focus on one thing single-mindedly

and see it through until it's done takes more character than anything else.

5. *Creativity.* Flood your life with ideas from many sources. Creativity needs to be exercised; like a muscle, if you don't use it, you'll lose it.

6. *Courage.* Most in demand and least in supply, courage is the willingness to do the things you know are right.

7. *Continuous learning.* Read at the very least one book a week . . . organize your time so you can spend 30 minutes a day exploring e-mail, sending messages, going through the Web sites, because it's like exercise. It's the only way you can keep on top of technology. If you get away from it, you'll lose your edge.[7]

Some people naively think the only important issue in leadership is character. I don't know how many sermons I've heard and books I've read that focus solely on the issue of character, believing simplistically that if you are the right kind of person, you will be an effective leader. However, we all know leaders who are spiritual giants but for whom no one likes to work. *They have integrity but not leadership skills.* Leadership is actually a complex set of gifts, skills, experience, and knowledge all working together. Like David, leaders must have a godly heart *and* proper skills.

But the fact that character is not the only thing does not mean it is not one of the most important. In fact character is absolutely essential, and it is a fundamental that cannot be compromised. We now turn in the next chapter to this issue of character and godliness.

3
THE PERSON
A Leader's Character

"But the LORD said to Samuel, 'Do not consider his appearance or his height, for I have rejected him. The LORD does not look at the things man looks at. Man looks at the outward appearance, but the LORD looks at the heart.'" (1 Sam. 16:7)

M Y PARENTS encouraged me to be a Cub Scout when I was a young boy. After Cub Scouts came Boy Scouts. In fact, they wouldn't let me quit Boy Scouts until I received my Eagle Award. Recently I ran across my Eagle Medal which I have had a little over thirty years. As a teenager I was embarrassed to have to stay in Scouts until I reached that milestone. As a high schooler I didn't think it was cool to be in Scouts. But when I became an adult, I can't count how many times I have been proud to say that I am an Eagle Scout. It means something, it stands for something, it cost me something to receive that award.

A few months ago I was rummaging through the basement of the house where I grew up. My father died fifteen years ago, but my mother still lives in that two-story homestead in Huntsville, Alabama. All the years we lived there, the basement workshop was my father's special domain. That's where he had his tools and where he "hung out" on Saturdays. The room is filled with memories, especially when I am in his workshop using his tools. When I think how many times he held those tools in his strong hands, it makes me well up with emotion—I sense a connection to him again though he is long gone.

I have a brother and a sister, both older than me, and the three of us work together to take care of our mom. Since I am somewhat practical with my hands, it has fallen to me to be the one to keep the house in shape and to fix the things that break. So I find myself still using the hammers, saw, screwdrivers, and even shop apron my father used for so many years. The nostalgic smells and sights are at times overwhelming. I miss him as much today as the day he died. So does my mother. I loved my father deeply, and I'm thankful for the character he imparted to me during his lifetime. I loved working with him and tinkering in his workshop. Like most young boys, I wanted to be like my dad.

Recently my ten-year-old son Andrew was by my side at my workbench in our basement. As I was busy fixing something, he found a small board and some nails and wanted to practice his hammering skills. The incident began as an irritation to me because he was distracting me from my goal of fixing what was broken so I could get on with the responsibilities of the evening. Raising four children has its stresses, and our evenings are always packed. This day happened to be right in the middle of the first week of school in the fall semester. Fortunately I caught myself and flashed back to all those times when I was able to be with my father in his workshop, and decided to relish the moment. I helped Andrew find some nails and continued the process of showing him how to drive nails with a heavy hammer. He enjoyed it and I enjoyed it; it was a special moment.

Rummaging through the basement that day not long ago at my childhood home, I found my old Cub Scout uniform. The tiny blue uniform is now over forty years old and is musty to say the least! It still has those cute little badges my mother lovingly sewed on the pockets and has the number of our pack sewn on the shoulder. I actually tried to put the uniform on, just for the sake of memories and nostalgia. What a joke! I am more than twice the size I was back then, just in sheer poundage. I decided to take the uniform home when I flew back to Chicago. I showed my piece of history to the kids and Andrew said immediately, "Dad, I want to try it on." He put it on and it fit—and the symbolism was complete. I was overwhelmed with emotion as I thought about me, my father, and now my youngest son and all the modeling and character impartation that can transfer from one generation to the next.

CHARACTER

"In reading the lives of great men," Harry Truman said, "I found that the first victory they won was over themselves. . . . Self-discipline with all of them came first."[1] Character is a number-one issue in leadership. In the words of John Maxwell, "Your gifts and skills might get you to the top, but only your character will keep you there."[2]

The knowledge that character is an important issue permeates the non-Christian world of leadership as well. Coach John Wooden, who led the UCLA Bruins basketball team to ten national titles in twelve years, emphasized character as the key to his success with his team: "Be more concerned with your character than with your reputation. Your character is what you really are while your reputation is merely what others think you are."[3]

The word *character* comes from a Latin word that means a mark or a distinctive quality. For example, one character in the alphabet is the letter *s*, which is unique from any other symbol. In terms of people and personalities, character is "one of the attributes or features that make up and distinguish an individual." Another definition I like is this: "The complex of mental and ethical traits marking and often individualizing a person, group or nation."[4] A person of good character is a person of moral excellence and soundness.

As we saw in chapter 2, David was chosen by God because of what the Lord saw in his heart. There was something about his character, even when he was a young shepherd, that God knew would serve him well throughout his life. David had one of the most unique relationships with his heavenly Father of any person in the Scriptures. God said he was "a man after my own heart" (Acts 13:22; see also 1 Sam. 13:14). He was committed to and concerned about the things that concern God. Presumably the converse was true as well; the Lord had an intense commitment to David as a leader. A few years later, when David wanted to build a temple for the Lord in Jerusalem, God reminded David of the Lord's blessings on his years of leadership. "Now then, tell my servant David, 'This is what the LORD Almighty says: I took you from the pasture and from following the flock to be ruler over my people Israel. I have been with you wherever you have gone and I have cut off all your enemies from before you. Now I will make your name great, like the names of the greatest men of the earth. And I will provide a place for my people Israel and will plant them so that they can have a home of their own and no longer be disturbed. Wicked people will not oppress them anymore, as they did at the beginning and have done ever since the time I appointed leaders over my people Israel. I will also give you rest from all your enemies' " (2 Sam. 7:8–11).

Then the Lord explained to David that he would not live to see the building of the sanctuary. His son Solomon would be the one to build the sanctuary on his behalf. I like David's response to God's promise that his son would build the temple and that his family line ("house") and kingdom would endure forever (7:11–16). Somewhat overwhelmed, he said, "Who am I, O Sovereign LORD, and what is my family, that you have brought me this far?" (7:18).

Haven't you said that to yourself sometime in your life? In those moments when you have felt unusually blessed by God and perhaps used by Him to influence others positively, haven't you asked, "Lord, why have you chosen me?"

The reason God chose David is that He knew David would "do everything I want him to do" (Acts 13:22).

MATTERS OF THE HEART

Integrity and character are just as crucial for effective leadership today as they were in the days of Israel. God is still looking for leaders like David, men and women willing to do whatever He asks of them.

Let's look at a few of the most important areas of concern. In the previous chapter we listed eight key functions of a leader in relation to his or her work: cultivating the vision, creating clear organization, choosing the right team, changing the culture, coaching the team, caring for the troops, curing the problems, and checking on progress.

Now let me suggest eight character qualities, based on my experience as a leader and my observations of other leaders.

Eight Qualities of Character

1. Purity of heart, mind, and hands (the problem of sin)
2. Posture of servanthood (the problem of pride)
3. Perseverance (the problem of follow-through)
4. Predictable and sustainable trust (the problem of integrity)
5. Promises kept and confidences held (the problem of confidence)
6. Partnership and parenthood (the problem of being faithful at home)
7. Prayer (the problem of intimacy with the Almighty)
8. Passion for Christ (the problem of sincerity)

PURITY OF HEART, MIND, AND HANDS
(THE PROBLEM OF SIN)

I admire people who are diligent in memorizing the Word of God. In my early years as a Christian I had no problem memorizing not only the Navigator's Topical Memory System but also dozens of lengthy passages of Scripture. But as the years have gone on, it has become a losing battle for me. Though I still rely heavily on passages I memorized years ago, my great desire is that I could improve my ability to memorize Scripture portions. I admire my father-in-law, Mark Bubeck, who in his seventies is still memorizing long Bible portions in his quiet time. My only consolation is that he no longer has a house full of children to raise and the intense, daily responsibilities of being a senior pastor as he had for forty years. However, even in the years he was a pastor, once the children were raised, he gave himself to memorizing Scripture.

Nothing gives us more power for purity than hiding God's Word in our hearts. The heart, the mind, and the hands are all protected by staying close to God's precepts. A psalmist wrote, "How can a young man keep his way pure? By living according to your word. I seek you with all my heart; do not let me stray from your commands. I have hidden your word in my heart that I might not sin against you" (Ps. 119:9–11).

One of my colleagues has memorized the following major portions of Scripture and has used them as continual calibration for his character. I find this is one of the best lists I have ever run across for working on issues of the heart. I highly recommend you commit these to memory too.

Target	Text	Goal
Heart	1 Corinthians	Love
Mind	Proverbs 3	Wisdom
Character	1 Timothy 3	Integrity
Purpose	Ephesians 4	Serving
Spirit	Philippians 4	Focus

A few years ago I asked my father-in-law, a man many people esteem for his spiritual integrity, prayer life, and purity, "Dad, of all the passages you've learned, memorized, and put in your heart through the years, what passages have made the greatest difference in your walking in victory in Jesus Christ?" Here's the list he gave me to work on; it is packed with spiritual power for daily living: Psalms 1, 27, 34, 91, 92, 139; Colossians 1:9–23; 2:6–15; and 3:1–17.

One final word on the power of God's Word, especially for us who are men, for we seem more prone to slip into moral impurity in our thought-life. In the summer of 1995, *Leadership Journal* published an entire issue on sins of moral impurity and the struggles of the flesh facing those in ministry. In that issue Jerry Kirk shared a list of Bible passages he has memorized. He says these eleven passages help him "move on the offensive against temptation."

Psalm 24:3–4: "Who may ascend the hill of the LORD? . . . He who has clean hands and a pure heart."

Psalm 101:2–3: "I will walk in my house with blameless heart. I will set before my eyes no vile thing."

Psalm 119:10: "Do not let me stray from your commands."

Matthew 4:4: "Man does not live on bread alone, but on every word that comes from the mouth of God."

Matthew 18:8: "If your hand or foot causes you to sin cut it off and throw it away."

Matthew 18:14: "Your Father in heaven is not willing that any of these little ones should be lost."

John 17:19: "For them I sanctify myself, that they too may be truly sanctified."

Ephesians 6:11: "Put on the full armor of God so that you can take your stand against the devil's schemes."

Hebrews 12:1: "Let us throw off everything that hinders and the sin that so easily entangles, and let us run with perseverance the race marked out for us."

1 John 3:8: "He who does what is sinful is of the devil."

1 John 4:4: "The one who is in you is greater than the one who is in the world."[5]

David was a failure in the area of purity; he committed adultery and murder. And yet God used him before and after the great moral failures of his life. "*Finishing strong* does not mean finishing unblemished," says Steve Farrar. And "finishing strong does not mean finishing perfect."[6]

Donna and I were privileged to pray with a godly woman who after years of personal and marital struggles came dangerously close to falling into adultery with another Christian man. The crisis is now past, and the Lord has healed her life and her marriage far beyond what she had ever dreamed possible. Although she acknowledged to us that the prayers of other believers were important to her victory, she surprised us with this statement: "In *the moment* of greatest temptation, even with opportunity and privacy available, what kept me from choosing sin was God's Word. The verses I had memorized as a child came to me, and I knew to be with this man would be direct disobedience to God." God has promised His

Word will not return to Him void! In the end, Scripture protected two Christian homes and countless others from devastation.

David could not shake the consequences of his sin. But he knew the way back to healing and forgiveness. What better chapter in all the Bible on the healing power of God's divine grace than Psalm 51:2–13?

> Wash away all my iniquity and cleanse me from my sin. For I know my transgressions, and my sin is always before me. Against you, you only, have I sinned and done what is evil in your sight, so that you are proved right when you speak and justified when you judge. Surely I was sinful at birth, sinful from the time my mother conceived me. Surely you desire truth in the inner parts; you teach me wisdom in the inmost place. Cleanse me with hyssop, and I will be clean; wash me, and I will be whiter than snow. Let me hear joy and gladness; let the bones you have crushed rejoice. Hide your face from my sins and blot out all my iniquity. Create in me a pure heart, O God, and renew a steadfast spirit within me. Do not cast me from your presence or take your Holy Spirit from me. Restore to me the joy of your salvation and grant me a willing spirit, to sustain me. Then I will teach transgressors your ways, and sinners will turn back to you.

POSTURE OF SERVANTHOOD
(THE PROBLEM OF PRIDE)

There is nothing about leadership that says we have to make people think we are powerful and important. On the contrary, servant leadership finds great strength in serving the needs of followers.

Many people still have the mistaken notion that leadership is being on the top of a pyramid where everyone else serves your needs and demands. Not so. Even secular management gurus are coming around to servant leadership, as we'll see in later chapters. Jesus taught a great lesson on the last night of His life on earth on what I call His "upside-down" approach to leadership. Servant leadership was very much on His mind as He wanted His key leaders to develop hearts of submission. It amazes me how the disciples acted even during the final hours Jesus spent with them! "Also a dispute arose among them as to which of them was considered to be greatest. Jesus said to them, 'The kings of the Gentiles lord it over them; and those who exercise authority over them call themselves Benefactors. But you are not to be like that. Instead, the greatest among you should be like the youngest, and the one who rules like the one who serves. . . . But I am among you as one who serves' " (Luke 22:24–27).

Top-down leadership is out of place in the church. Even in the secular world today's workers, employees, and volunteers expect to be a part of the decision-making process in organizations in which they are involved. Effective leaders have closed the distance between leader and follower, coming out of closed-off mahogany executive suites and into the open office world of the workers. Even Andrew Grove, chief executive officer of Intel, works in an eight-foot by nine-foot cubicle in his corporate head-quarters in Silicon Valley, California. Leadership accessibility and teamwork are the buzzwords of the nineties.

A servant leader sees his or her role quite differently from the tradi-tional top-down dictator type. The servant leader is there to make the worker successful, not vice versa. Our workers and/or employees are hired to serve not us, but the mission of our church or organization. Our role as their leader is to facilitate their effectiveness in any way we can, much as a coach tries to get optimum performance out of his team players.

Our Lord modeled and taught this style of servant leadership right up to the night He was betrayed, even washing the feet of His disciples to demonstrate servanthood. "Now that I, your Lord and Teacher, have washed your feet, you also should wash one another's feet. I have set you an example that you should do as I have done for you" (John 13:14–15).

Gordon MacDonald's excellent book on Christian character develop-ment, *The Life God Blesses*, has great lessons on tending the soul. He develops these according to his imagery of sailing and what goes on "un-der the waterline." He believes that one of the prerequisites to spirituality is submission: "I am blunt to say . . . that people cannot hope to possess spirituality if they seek to avoid that covenantal relationship called sub-mission."[7]

Servant leaders must be willing to live lives filled with submission on many levels: submission to authority, submission to God the Father, sub-mission to one's spouse, submission to the principles of wise living, and submission to one's obligations. Though conventional wisdom says everyone should submit to their leaders, the *real truth is that leaders, to be effective, must learn to submit.*

One of the most serious character flaws to mar the effectiveness of a leader is a subtle spiritual pride in this area of authority. The leaders I have observed with this flaw have a pattern of being unable to submit to authority throughout their years of ministry. This blind spot can severely limit the full potential of gifted leaders. Effective leaders think of the collective wisdom of elders or of a board of directors as the "checks and balances" of their overall leadership. An inability or refusal to submit in this way is evidence of a subtle spirit of arrogance and unhealthy self-sufficiency. We must be certain, as leaders, to constantly keep before us the example of our Lord Jesus, who always acknowledged openly his submission to the Father's will. As leaders we must submit to authority, even if at times we disagree with those who are our "checks and balances." Leaders who follow Christ's example of submission demonstrate to their followers a powerful pattern they in turn will want to follow.

Since the leader is the keeper of the culture, it falls on his or her shoulders to cultivate a culture that is distinctly Christian. Whatever values and beliefs that leader holds usually become the assumptions of the followers. That puts great responsibility on the shoulders of a servant leader. Christian leaders should strive to model servant leadership that is distinct from the traditional top-down secular corporate model.

PERSEVERANCE
(THE PROBLEM OF FOLLOW-THROUGH)

Back in 1986 I ran my one and only marathon—in beautiful Vienna, Austria. After months of training in the Vienna woods, I was within three weeks of the great day of the race. One Saturday my friends and I ran sixteen miles from our office, over the hills to the home of a friend in a neighboring village. We were to meet our wives and children there for an early evening picnic with our families. I barely made it. I "hit the wall." When I arrived, Donna said I looked sickly green and completely exhausted. I wanted to quit. "I'm not going through with it," I told her in despair. "Forget the marathon; it was a stupid idea!"

During all my months of training Donna had thought it was a questionable pursuit, but now at this moment so close to the end she turned 180 degrees: "No way are you quitting now!" she declared. I needed her strength, and I did go on and finish my training. I persevered, and on the day of the race I finished the Vienna Marathon in three hours and fifty minutes, meeting my goal of beating four hours.

Leadership often boils down to 95 percent perspiration and 5 percent inspiration. There is no substitute for prolonged faithfulness in sticking to the tasks God has given us to perform. Perseverance through suffering, criticism, and the hardships that come with leadership is a key character ingredient for the task. *When everyone else is ready to quit, you as the leader must go on.*

The Greek word *hypomoneμ* occurs thirty-one times in the New Testament, with the NIV usually rendering it "perseverance" or "endurance." This word usually reflects the trait of a mature disciple of Jesus. Romans 5 and James 1 both directly correlate perseverance to proven character: "Not only so, but we also rejoice in our sufferings, because we know that suffering produces perseverance; perseverance, character; and character, hope" (Rom. 5:3–4). "Because you know that the testing of your faith develops perseverance. Perseverance must finish its work so that you may be mature and complete, not lacking anything" (James 1:3–4).

Perseverance was one of the key traits many leaders of old possessed. "Therefore, since we are surrounded by such a great cloud of witnesses, let us throw off everything that hinders and the sin that so easily entangles, and let us run with perseverance the race marked out for us" (Heb.12:1).

Mature leaders can endure delayed gratification—the ability to persevere, to see something through even when everyone else grows tired and weary; they delay short-term gratification to maximize the long-term gain.

PREDICTABLE AND SUSTAINABLE TRUST
(THE PROBLEM OF INTEGRITY)

When anyone asks me to recommend some good books on leadership, one that always comes to the top of my list is *Leaders: The Strategies for Taking Charge* by Warren Bennis and Burt Nanus. In their chapter on "Trust through Positioning," two profound sentences summarize the long-term endurance of an effective leader: "Trust is the emotional glue that binds followers and leaders together. The accumulation of trust is a measure of the legitimacy of leadership."[8]

Without a doubt, trust is the glue that holds together all human organizations. I remember several situations when I was involved with an organization in which trust broke down. These remind me a lot of the spirit that must have prevailed on the *Titanic* during its last hours. All hope was abandoned; panic had set in. Faith in the captain had vanished, and every person had to fend for himself. Moments like that are times of great despair, distrust, and anger, and mark the onset of personal survival ambition. Haven't many of us experienced this in a local church when factions and divisions have developed? A leadership crisis always eliminates trust and what takes its place is not a pretty sight.

The dictionary definition of integrity is "an unimpaired condition" or "the quality or state of being complete or undivided."[9] Integrity builds trust in followers to the point that the organization is *unimpaired* and able to forge ahead successfully.

Bennis and Nanus discuss two key ingredients that must be sustained between a leader and a follower. Without these two, leadership cannot be sustained. First, a leader's *vision* for the organization must be clear, attractive, and attainable. We tend to trust leaders who create these visions, since visions represent the context for shared beliefs in a common organizational purpose. Second, a leader's *positions* must be clear. We tend to trust leaders when we know where they stand in relation to the organization and how they position the organization relative to the environment.[10]

PROMISES KEPT AND CONFIDENCES HELD
(THE PROBLEM OF CONFIDENCE)

How good is your word? Is your credibility such that your followers can move ahead, knowing you won't change your course midstream? Are you known as someone who is reliable in doing what you say you will do? Reliable leaders keep their promises. That trait often separates leaders from followers. Jesus may have had this in mind when He said, "Well done, good and faithful servant! You have been faithful with a few things;

I will put you in charge of many things. Come and share your master's happiness!" (Matt. 25:21).

Along with keeping promises we must keep confidences. Our mission recently faced a major issue that required strict confidentiality. For the information to leak out prematurely would have been destructive to many people and to the organization. I watched with interest as we on the leadership team committed to share the information only with our spouses. I'm proud to say that the group kept a tight lid on the information for several months. When it finally did leak out, it was not through my team but from another person who was in on the secret but could not keep it to himself. He "confidentially" told a good friend, who was asked not to repeat it, who in turn told his friend in "confidence" not to repeat it. That is not keeping confidences; passing along privileged information is breaking trust. That person really let us down. Fortunately the damage was minimal, as the time was near for the information to be released.

Don't give out confidential information entrusted to you. The temptation to share the power of confidential information is great, but the reward of being known as a person who can be trusted is far greater.

James summed up this quality of trustworthiness: "Above all, my brothers, do not swear—not by heaven or by earth or by anything else. Let your 'Yes' be yes, and your 'No,' no, or you will be condemned" (James 5:12). Don't say yes to something when in reality you have no intention of doing it, when you have no authority or ability to do it, when you may change your mind and are not really committed to following through, or when the time and resources at your disposal will not allow you to do it.

PARTNERSHIP AND PARENTHOOD
(THE PROBLEM OF FAITHFULNESS AT HOME)

Many great leaders have been successful in the eyes of the public but have failed miserably in the eyes of their loved ones. A leader, if married, must make his or her commitment to and nurturing of the marriage relationship a top priority. Paul made that clear in Ephesians 5:22–33, where he exhorted both husbands and wives to fulfill their responsibilities. It still baffles me to see leaders in the Christian world who justify putting ministry before all else because they believe ministry alone is God's work and therefore must have first priority. *Being a faithful and nurturing spouse is a significant part of God's work!*

Along with this responsibility to be a good spouse comes the issue of raising children in a godly, loving, healthy home. Of the parental responsibilities of leaders (overseers and deacons), Paul wrote, "He must manage his own family well and see that his children obey him with proper respect. (If anyone does not know how to manage his own family, how can he take care of God's church?) . . . A deacon must be the husband of but one wife and must manage his children and his household well" (1 Tim. 3:4–5, 12).

As a newlywed student at Dallas Seminary, I well remember the impact Howard Hendricks had on me. He told us that when he left the seminary at the end of each day he left his work behind. Hendricks said he crossed a bridge every day going to and from the seminary. Each day he would mentally toss everything related to his work over the bridge on his way home and was thus free to give his full attention to his family. The following morning he would mentally pick up those work responsibilities and be ready to face a new day.

This concept is not always easy to follow. But if you have no relationship with your family and work is always first in your time and attention, then in the words of radio talk-show host, Dr. Laura Schlessinger, "You're nothing more than a worker ant." That is, you could be replaced in the hearts and lives of your family by "hired help." As difficult as it was to commit myself to this principle, I have done it. I began it as a seminary student, committing myself always to go to bed at the same time as Donna, and by disciplining my time, I did that. Thus my work does not own me! Today, after practicing this principle for more than twenty-three years, I think the results in my marriage and children are evident. Donna and I have a great marriage, and at least most of the time she knows where she stands in my life. Our children know that when I am home, I am available to them.

I realize that many pastors have interruptions of crisis proportions and receive important phone calls from their people. Yet their stance in general should be such that their families know that in spite of ministry interruptions, they come first. Donna and her sisters are "PKs" (pastor's kids) who did *not* grow up to resent the ministry (as so many PKs do), precisely because her father knew how to balance the weight of a large ministry well. He pastored large churches, and was in demand as a counselor, taking at least five phone calls a day at home from people around the world because of his books on spiritual warfare and prayer. Yet his children and his wife knew they were his first priority, and all of them today are joyfully serving the Lord in ministry or lay leadership responsibilities.

Sometimes the heroic leaders of days gone by can surprise us with their soft side. Certainly General Douglas MacArthur, who led American troops in both World War II and the Korean War, was a rough and tough leader. But here is what he said about how he wanted his son to remember him: "By profession I'm a soldier and take pride in that fact. But I am prouder—infinitely prouder—to be a father. A soldier destroys in order to build; the father only builds, never destroys. The one has the potentiality of death; the other embodies creation and life. And while the hordes of death are mighty, the battalions of life are mightier still. It is my hope that my son, when I am gone, will remember me not from the battle but in the home repeating with him our simple daily prayer, 'Our Father, who art in heaven.' "[11]

PRAYER
(THE PROBLEM OF INTIMACY WITH THE ALMIGHTY)

In Henry Blackaby's recent book, *The Power of the Call*, he lists a number of spiritual qualifications for leadership. Among them is an *absolute priority and commitment to prayer*. "There is no possibility of a person being a spiritual leader who does not understand the absolute priority and urgency of being a person of prayer. Prayer is a relationship with God where, in His Presence, He reveals who He is and what He is about. You then can have a sensitive heart that reaches out to God. . . ."[12]

The subject of prayer can be one of Christendom's greatest sources of guilt. It should not be so, but many of us feel more failure in this area than in any other pursuit in the Christian life. David modeled a life of prayer, as seen in the Book of Psalms. No one can read the Psalms without being lifted up into the very presence of God. This great book of praise and prayer revealed David's high commitment to intimacy with the Almighty. For example, "For the LORD is righteous, he loves justice; upright men will see his face" (Ps. 11:7). "I sought the LORD, and he answered me; he delivered me from all my fears. Those who look to him are radiant; their faces are never covered with shame. This poor man called, and the LORD heard him; he saved him out of all his troubles" (34:4–6).

Paul too admonished us about the importance of prayer. "I urge, then, first of all, that requests, prayers, intercession and thanksgiving be made for everyone—for kings and all those in authority, that we may live peaceful and quiet lives in all godliness and holiness. This is good, and pleases God our Savior" (1 Tim. 2:1–3).

Paul emphasized that it would take discipline to accomplish this life of depth and godliness. "For physical training is of some value, but godliness has value for all things, holding promise for both the present life and the life to come" (4:8).

> *Prayer must be the oxygen of the spiritual life of a Christian leader.*

Without it, intimacy with God is lost, and character will fail. Jesus modeled this best. His walk of prayer and intimacy with God the Father marked His every move in His earthly ministry. How much more must we pray! We must pray both to hear God's heart, but we must also pray for those we lead, as did Jesus in His prayer for us in John 17. "My prayer is not for the world, but for those you have given me, because they belong to you" (17:9, NLT).

In his gracious manner Richard Foster, in his great book on character, *Celebration of Discipline*, nails us for the lack of time we give to the inner feeding of our souls. His gentle rebuke is worth noting: "Superficiality is the curse of our age. The doctrine of instant satisfaction is a primary spiritual problem. The desperate need today is not for a greater number of intelligent people or gifted people, but for deep people."[13]

PASSION FOR CHRIST
(THE PROBLEM OF SINCERITY)

David's final charge to his son Solomon mirrors what he valued as most important. A man's dying words are lasting words. Here's how David exhorted Solomon from his deathbed: "When the time drew near for David to die, he gave a charge to Solomon his son. 'I am about to go the way of all the earth,' he said. 'So be strong, show yourself a man, and observe what the LORD your God requires: Walk in his ways, and keep his decrees and commands, his laws and requirements, as written in the Law of Moses, so that you may prosper in all you do and wherever you go, and that the LORD may keep his promise to me: "If your descendants watch how they live, and if they walk faithfully before me with all their heart and soul, you will never fail to have a man on the throne of Israel"'" (1 Kings 2:1–4).

David had an insatiable appetite to know God as displayed in Psalm 42:1–2. "As the deer pants for streams of water, so my soul pants for you, O God. My soul thirsts for God, for the living God. When can I go and meet with God?" Charles Spurgeon said this of David's longing for God: "David was heartsick. Ease he did not seek, honor he did not covet, but the enjoyment of communion with God was an urgent need of his soul . . . an absolute necessity, like water to a stag . . . his soul, his very self, his deepest life was insatiable for a sense of the divine presence. . . . O to have the most intense craving after the highest good."[14]

Sometimes we think of passion as a fire that burns out quickly. But to me spiritual passion runs deep: It is a lifelong commitment to follow the disciplines necessary to achieve and sustain spirituality. In the words of Gordon MacDonald, "Nothing of value is ever acquired without discipline."[15] As he describes the lessons we can learn from the spiritual masters of days gone by, and their passion for God, MacDonald observes, "They have warned us that the one who would get in touch with the soul must do so with diligence and determination. One must overcome feelings, fatigue, distractions, errant appetites, and popular opinion."[16]

How impeccable can we expect to be as leaders? We do ourselves and others harm by expecting to be perfect and portraying the image that we have everything together. It is no accident that we know all about the blemishes and sins of our Bible heroes. As Billy Graham explains, "Standards of lifestyle and conduct for those in the Christian ministry are rooted in the Old Testament patriarchs, leaders and prophets. They were approved by God for the way they lived. That did not mean they were perfect. The Bible is absolutely honest about their sins and failure. It records these, sometimes in embarrassing detail, so that we may learn from them and avoid their failures."[17]

In 1996, on the occasion of the fortieth anniversary of the founding of Christianity Today, Inc., Billy Graham took a few moments to reflect on the past and future of evangelicalism. Regarding the past, he made the interesting observation that we certainly would not have predicted the progress evangelicalism has made over these four decades. We've made tremendous strides, not only here in North America but around the world, in spreading the gospel, establishing effective local churches, and building literally thousands of fruitful ministries.

But speaking of the future, Billy Graham sounded a strong word of caution. Though he is optimistic, he believes the future impact of evangelicals will depend on six factors, each of which has a lot to do with character.

> *First, the evangelical future will depend on our vision.* The twin enemies of vision are always complacency and discouragement. Complacency makes us lazy; discouragement paralyzes us. Few things cripple us like pride and self-satisfaction in the face of success, or despair in the face of evil. . . .
>
> *Second, it will depend on our trust.* . . . But will we fight the spiritual battles of the future in the energy of the flesh? Or will we yield ourselves to the power of the Holy Spirit; using the spiritual weapons God has provided to combat the forces of evil arrayed against us? . . .
>
> *Third, it will depend on our obedience.* Few things discredit the gospel in the eyes of the world more quickly than moral and ethical failure by those claiming to follow Christ. . . . Satan apparently does not need to invent any new temptations; the allures of money, pleasure and power seem quite sufficient to blunt our witness and neutralize our impact. . . .

Fourth, it will depend on our love and compassion. Just as moral compromise blunts our message, so does an unloving or indifferent spirit. Divine love sent Christ into the world, and that same love must compel us to reach out to a hurting and torn world. ...

Fifth, it will depend on our faithfulness to the Word of God. ... Will we lose confidence in [the Bible's] trustworthiness intentionally or unintentionally looking elsewhere for spiritual foundations? ... We must seek to be faithful to the Word of God, allowing it to shape our thinking and mold our behavior.

Finally, the future impact of evangelicals will depend on our steadfastness. ... We are called to be steadfast for Christ and his truth, regardless of the situation. Our calling is not to be successful (as the world measures success); our calling is to be faithful.[18]

Filling the shoes of leadership is always a big job. At times we may get so confused about our priorities that a list like this is a good reminder. Keeping the main things the main things is important for leaders. Another man of great impact today in his leadership is Charles R. Swindoll, who told a local newspaper a few years ago that he credits his success as a leader to a "strong family, many good friends and a simple lifestyle." "My job," he says, "is to set the vision, to say 'thank you' and to keep walking in purity."[19]

4
ENCOURAGEMENT

Empowering Those You Lead

"Therefore encourage one another and build each other up, just as in fact you are doing." (1 Thess. 5:11)

THE CITY OF CALCUTTA can best be described with one word: *squalor.* I have never visited a city so filled with human misery. On a tour of the city several years ago, I drove through the streets in a taxi. My lungs were quickly clogged by the terrible smog and smoke from the small fires all along the streets where people were preparing their dinners. Calcutta has not just a few blocks of highly depressed poverty, but mile after depressing mile of people living in cardboard boxes on the streets and bathing in the open sewers. As I looked at the seemingly endless human suffering I asked the Lord this question: "How could one person, even if he spent his whole life pouring himself out for the needs of this city, make any dent at all?"

My answer came the next morning when I had the opportunity to meet Mother Teresa at her headquarters in the sprawling Sisters of Mercy complex. The first thing I noticed were her feet; she was barefoot because of a deformity that made shoes very painful for her to wear. Then her height impressed me—the lack thereof! I wondered how such a little frail woman could win a Nobel prize. As we spoke and I toured her ministry center, I saw what one willing person has accomplished in the midst of so much misery. In spite of my differences with many doctrines and teachings of the Roman Catholic Church, I was moved by the impact of this tiny woman's life. I can say with confidence that every outreach to those desperate people in Calcutta (as well as all over India) that is having a lasting impact on that nation and is meeting urgent needs is being done in the name of Jesus Christ.

Mother Teresa impressed me deeply with her gift of encouragement. During the few minutes we were together, she asked questions about me. When she found out I was from Chicago, she told me about her wonderful visit to Chicago and what a great city it is. Then she quoted several verses of Scripture to me, and I realized as I walked away that her mission with me was to give me *personal encouragement*. At no time during our brief encounter was attention focused on her and all she has accomplished.

Rarely has one person provided so much radiance and encouragement in such hopeless misery. And she and her sisters don't just talk about meeting needs; they do it. They have provided homes, food, shelter, and clothing to tens of thousands of orphans, widows, homeless people, and ex-prostitutes. Through her gift of encouragement Mother Teresa will always be remembered as one of the great leaders of the twentieth century. She is sorely missed in India.

"Encouragement is oxygen to the soul," remarked George Adams many years ago. Some things never change, and giving positive feedback for a job well done has always and will always be very much a part of leading. Encouragement is one of the strongest weapons we have in our arsenals of influence. Jesus spoke of its importance when in a parable a master said to his servant, "Well done, good and faithful servant! You have been faithful with a few things; I will put you in charge of many things. Come and share your master's happiness!" (Matt. 25:21). Leadership is very much about supplying those oxygen lines to our followers. And I have never met a leader who did not also need encouragement along the way.

For years I have kept an encouragement notebook. It now fills several thick three-ring binders, not because I have done so much for which people have encouraged me, but because I save every one of those precious good strokes when I get them. I am amazed at how God brings a note or word of encouragement at just the right time when He knows I need it. Recently I was feeling discouraged about some criticism I had received. A card of encouragement arrived in the mail from the wife of one of our staff leaders. It had a great healing effect on my soul. It read:

This is a note to let you know that it is 5:30 A.M. and I have been praying for you. You may be feeling down right now—Phil and I know that feeling also—I am praying for you to feel the shield of faith. When we are discouraged those fiery darts seem to get bigger and faster. Phil and I are not unaware of the big responsibilities you carry. We are so thankful for your leadership at CBI. Remember Joshua 1:9, "Have I not commanded you? Be strong and courageous. Do not be terrified, do not be discouraged, for the Lord your God will be with you wherever you go." Philippians 4:19, "And my God will meet all your needs" is our prayer for you this day,

Love, Diane

I needed that. This kind of word is like an oasis in the desert for anyone who receives it. All kinds of things produce deserts in our lives, including illness, criticism, failure, grief, idleness, stress, and strained relationships.

Encouragement is one of the premier functions of leadership. I have come to believe strongly that *people can never be encouraged too much.* The world we live in is full of so many discouraging things. I deeply appreciate the people who have encouraged me through the years and made the effort to let me know when I've done a good job. Donna and I have committed ourselves to encouraging our children. There are always plenty of people to beat them down, to tell them they don't measure up and that they're not good enough. I try to encourage my four children when they exhibit positive qualities. We carefully balance encouragement, acceptance, and love with discipline, as we are seeking to raise them to love and follow the Lord, and to discover all He has planned for their lives.

A LIFE ON THE LINE

It means a great deal to our followers if we are leading from the front, not pushing from behind. Are we willing to be out there with them in the trenches, not sitting back in nice offices calling the commands via e-mail, fax, and voice mail? Leaders need to be on the front lines of the battle. We have to take the heat for where our leadership is taking our church or the organization. It is up to us to stand up to the opponents of our plans, not to send others to take the heat. We're the ones who often have to take the bullets and the explosions that are thrown at the front line. Remember, leaders lead; they don't push followers from behind.

Esther was just such a leader. She is one of the great female leaders in God's redemptive story—a heroine who stepped on center stage for a fleeting time, just long enough to show us what courageous, encouraging leadership is all about. Esther was willing to put her life on the line and risk perishing for the good of her people.

God led Esther to a position of incredible greatness in leadership at a crucial moment in the history of His people, the Jews. Leadership is not only a long-term practice; at times it is a momentary act in a particular situation, which will have lifelong, broad impact. Sometimes great leadership lasts for only a moment—but a crucial moment for all involved. Esther rose from obscurity in God's providence to be used at a moment in history when she was needed. When her time came, she was available, and she rose to the challenge. That's leadership.

Every leader has weeks, months, or years of obscurity. In those times we may feel we're useless and that God has forgotten us. But God is preparing us for the moments when He needs us.

Esther, whose story is recorded in the Old Testament book with her name, was a beautiful woman. In fact she rose to prominence and was used in a leadership position partly because of her physical beauty. God uses many different gifts and endowments for His purposes, and in her case He used her outward beauty and her inward integrity to save His people. The story of Esther revolves around the mighty king Xerxes who ruled over 127 provinces stretching from India to North Africa during the heyday of the Persian Empire. He ruled for twenty years, from 485 to 465 B.C.

Leaders usually have opponents; we can count on it. In this case his name was Haman. Haman hated the Jews and planned a conspiracy to have Xerxes decree the destruction of every Israelite in the Persian kingdom. Esther, whose Jewish nationality was not known to the king, became queen through an elaborate selection process in which she was chosen because of her beauty and demeanor. Mordecai, the hero in this story, had adopted Esther, a close relative, when her own father and mother died (Esth. 2:7).

At the crucial moment in this drama, when evil Haman had persuaded Xerxes to decree the death of all the Jews, Mordecai approached Esther with the great leadership challenge of her life. "Do not think that because you are in the king's house you alone of all the Jews will escape. For if you remain silent at this time, relief and deliverance for the Jews will arise from another place, but you and your father's family will perish. *And who knows but that you have come to royal position for such a time as this?*" (4:13–14, italics added).

At times leadership boils down to this simple challenge: Will we rise to the opportunity placed before us? We are often asked to do things we don't think we're capable of and to fulfill responsibilities we feel inadequate for. How inadequate and incapable did Esther feel on that day? Look at the odds that were stacked against her: She must have been greatly afraid, not only of losing her own life, but of seeing all her relatives and her entire race annihilated. She could have said to herself, "I didn't ask for this. This is not my problem. Let somebody else do it!" Great leaders surely think those thoughts, but then they lay them aside as she did and rise to the occasion. This situation must have been one of both fear and faith: fear of what could happen to her if she didn't respond, but faith that God would provide a way of escape.

Aware that the king was the most powerful man in the region, Esther certainly must have feared him, especially knowing the fate of her predecessor, Queen Vashti. Certainly she was in a position of great vulnerability. But Esther sent this reply to Mordecai's challenge: "Go, gather together all the Jews who are in Susa, and fast for me. Do not eat or drink for three days, night or day. I and my maids will fast as you do. When this is done, I will go to the king, even though it is against the law [no one, unless summoned by the king, was allowed to approach him, under penalty of death]. *And if I perish, I perish*" (4:16, italics added).

In an unlikely set of events we find one of the great stories of victory in the Bible. The five words, "If I perish, I perish," have become known throughout history as an expression of Esther's faith. In fact it is not only a story of faith and subsequent victory, but also a story of sweet revenge as Haman was hanged and his nemesis, Mordecai, was given the greatest honor of the kingdom. And Esther asked the king to spare not only her life but also the lives of all her people, and he did so.

Haman was hanged on the seventy-five-foot-high gallows he had built in hopes of hanging Mordecai. Then the king declared an edict on behalf of the Jews, which gave them the right in every city to assemble and protect themselves, to destroy, kill, and annihilate any armed forces of any nationality that might attack them. This decree established the Jews' safety and security in the region. Then the Jews throughout the empire had a joyous celebration. "For the Jews it was a time of happiness and joy, gladness and honor. In every province and in every city, wherever the edict of the king went, there was joy and gladness among the Jews, with feasting and celebrating. And many people of other nationalities became Jews because fear of the Jews had seized them" (8:16–17).

What an encouragement Esther was as a leader for her people. How would the people have felt had she tried to save only herself? They would have been without hope, in despair, helpless victims. She rose to the occasion, and as a result she is known as a great heroine.

To encourage means providing courage for our followers.

This beautiful queen reminds me of a modern-day princess whose short life was filled with acts of encouragement for the suffering and downtrodden. Esther's actions call to mind the courage that is captured in this often-quoted verse that Princess Diana used in many of her speeches:

> Life is mostly froth and bubble,
> Two things stand in stone:
> Kindness in another's trouble,
> Courage in your own.[1]

ENCOURAGEMENT COSTS

Leaders need to dispense encouragement freely and often. But who encourages the encouragers? A pastor wrote to me about the issue of loneliness, and I think it speaks so well to this painful part of leadership that many people don't fully appreciate.

While I have personally tried to be vulnerable and transparent from the pulpit and with individuals, there is indeed a deep personal sense of loneliness that comes from being at the top. I have noticed over the years that my associates are able to enjoy relationships with one another that I am prevented from personally being able to enjoy with any of them beyond a certain point. I believe this has something to do with where the buck stops. Somebody has to make the hard calls. A leader who is not willing to make those hard calls no longer serves his or her church and/or organization well.

Sincerely, Dan

I've seen this in my own ministry. As a leader I must represent everyone's interests, not just the interest of the person who happens to be in my office. I can't have close ties with everyone. I have to hold confidences that I cannot share freely even with my closest friends. Then I have in my hands the control of people's finances, benefits, and personal futures because of my role in the administration. Frankly, people know that a pastor or a leader of an organization really has ultimate control over the destiny of his staff, which puts a natural distance in the relationship.

Probably the best place leaders can find encouragement is outside of their organization. As I talk to many leaders, they seem without fail to have close friends outside their system. With them you can speak candidly, share "horror stories," and lay your worst fears and frustrations on the table safely. Be sure to find a source of encouragement for yourself, or you will not be able to be a supply of encouragement for others.

Being involved in pastoral leadership is an assignment that has much to do with shepherding, as Peter wrote. "Be shepherds of God's flock that is under your care, serving as overseers—not because you must, but because you are willing, as God wants you to be; not greedy for money but eager to serve; not lording it over those entrusted to you, but being examples to the flock" (1 Pet. 5:2–3).

As churches have grown larger and senior pastors have become more stressed out, some people are saying that pastors of larger churches should be ranchers rather than shepherds. The rancher makes sure the sheep are taken care of, but doesn't have personal contact with all of them. This concept has probably been more harmful than beneficial. You may not be able to make a personal pastoral call on everyone in your congregation, but they must sense that you personally care about them.

In my own role this has been a struggle, for we have hundreds of people involved in our ministry scattered all over the world. No matter how busy I am, I must make sure that people sense that I care for them every time I have contact with them. I need to make sure that somewhere along the road I have a chance to have a personal conversation with each of them. *Great leaders make everyone they come in contact with feel important.* A leader of a larger church or organization really does not have the time to get close to everyone who works with them, but it is important to have a caring concern for each individual.

> **People don't care how much you know until they know how much you care.**

The personal encouragement of a busy leader came home to me personally out of the ashes of a tragic fire our family experienced. One of my closest friends, Dennis, ministered to my heart in a way I have rarely seen. In the summer of 1994 our family enjoyed an extended vacation in the Colorado Rockies in our motor home. This "home away from home" was for myself, Donna, and our four children our "memory maker." We loved to get away and make family memories at various campgrounds. On the last day of our vacation, just five hours from home, cruising along Interstate 80 in central Iowa, the engine of our motor home caught fire. We didn't actually know it was on fire until the engine died and we stopped. Once we came to a complete stop, flames leaped out from under the hood and engulfed the front of the vehicle. We quickly evacuated the family (and our dog Taffy), and I began the futile task of trying to put out the hot blazing engine fire. Many people stopped, jumped out of their cars and trucks with their own fire extinguishers, and tried to lend a hand in the battle.

Fighting the fire that day was futile, and in the end we watched our motor home and all its memories burn to the frame. That moment is one of the saddest days in our family's memory. Others have experienced much worse; but for us, it was traumatic as we watched our beautiful summer memories and many possessions go up in smoke.

A week later I decided to return to the burned-out hull of the motor home to see if I could salvage anything. The insurance company had already written it off as a total loss. There were a few important memories that I had hoped would perhaps have escaped the fire. When I set out on the long journey to return to the scene of the accident, my friend Dennis volunteered to go along. We spent a whole day driving out and rummaging through the wreckage. In the back I found Donna's Bible, my Bible, and my journal! Although they were charred on the edges, and had the strong smell of that kind of fire, not one word was missing from any of our Bibles, or my journal. My journal was irreplaceable; it included my father's handwritten eulogy, which I had read at his funeral. I am so glad I recovered it. We sifted through the charred, burned-out hull and molten mass of destroyed possessions for probably four hours.

When it was over, Dennis and I looked at each other and broke into laughter. We looked like a couple of chimney sweepers desperately in need of a shower! We were covered with soot from head to toe. Even though the background of this day was filled with tragedy, it was a day of great encouragement for me. My friend Dennis, a busy man with his own life and leadership responsibilities, took a day out of his life to go with me to do something difficult in a moment when he knew I was really hurting. I'll never forget that time when he mentored me as an older brother in Christ and demonstrated what it means to encourage one another.

A lot of people where I live know Dennis. I am amazed at how often when his name comes up people say, "He helped me move last year," or, "He hooked up our washer and dryer the day we moved." He is the kind of friend who will help you fix your car, move your furniture, or cry with you in moments of tragedy. That day Dennis taught me much about caring for people. He taught me that it costs; it cost him a whole day out of his life. And he taught me there is nothing more powerful in leadership than showing genuine caring concern for those who are in pain. He is a leader who knows how to be effective in the ministry of encouragement.

HOW TO ENCOURAGE

It is unlikely that we will be called to save our people from extinction as Esther was challenged to do. But every leader can assume the important role of encouragement. So how do we go about this ministry of encouragement? Actually, *knowing* how to encourage is not a difficult science; it is *doing* it that comes hard for busy leaders. And encouragement must be done over and over and over again. "One of the commodities in life that most people can't get enough of is compliments. The ego is never so intact that one can't find a hole in which to plug a little praise. But, compliments by their very nature are highly biodegradable and tend to dissolve hours or days after we receive them—which is why we can always use another."[2]

The apostle Paul knew how to encourage, even though he was a busy leader. He had the type of personality we may not associate with caring, warm, personal leadership, but here is what he wrote: "But we were gentle among you, like a mother caring for her little children. We loved you so much that we were delighted to share with you not only the gospel of God but our lives as well, because you had become so dear to us" (1 Thess. 2:7–8).

How do we go about a ministry of encouragement? There are many ways to encourage the people in our care, but I will focus on five key elements.

Five Ways to Encourage Followers

1. Encourage with attention.
2. Encourage when crisis comes.
3. Encourage when a job is well done.
4. Encourage when they do poorly.
5. Encourage whenever there is opportunity.

Encourage with Attention: Listening and Learning

Parenting includes many parallels to leadership in the working world. Ruth Bell Graham raised the Graham children with lots of love and encouragement, and as a good leader must do, she did not pretend to be perfect herself or to expect her children to be without fault. She wrote about how important listening is in the process of encouragement. "If I cannot give my children a perfect mother, I can at least give them more of the one they've got—and make that one more loving. I will be available. I will take time to listen, time to play, time to be home when they arrive from school, time to counsel and encourage."[3]

How many nights do we lie on our teenagers' beds listening to them pour out their hearts as they are processing the world into which they are growing? The more people you lead, the more you must listen. That is why God gave us two ears but only one mouth. *Effective leadership has more to do with listening than with talking.* Some days I get worn out listening to the problems my staff bring me. Even when I don't feel like listening to one more issue, I realize that leadership demands it and that they deserve it from me. How can I know what is going on in the church or in my organization if I am not listening? If I am not listening to them, I can be sure they will go elsewhere to be heard, and that may become destructive and not for the good of the whole ministry.

Leaders by their very nature tend to be removed from the front lines of battle in the organization. Therefore they must listen to those in the trenches, relying on that information to make wise decisions.

The greatest innovations and strides forward we will make in our calling will arise from ideas generated at the fringes of our organization.

We don't have all the answers about our future; often we don't even know many of the questions. But answers often come from those doing the work. And how will we leaders ever harvest those profound ideas if we do not listen long, hard, and often? Leaders who try to preserve the status quo close themselves off and listen to only those voices that agree with them. But learning leaders listen—and listening leaders learn. The first step in the ministry of encouragement comes from being a listening leader.[4]

Encourage When Crisis Comes

We saw how Esther rose to the occasion of courageous leadership in a time of great national crisis. It is during those times in your organization that people learn your character and what you are made of. About two years after I became the head of CBI, a huge financial crisis hit us. It had the potential to ruin us and to cost me my job as leader. By God's grace we finally managed to weather the storm. For a few days in that dark valley I thought my leadership position was over. But now that I look back, I see that God used that crisis to help me grow, and I was also able to be an encouragement to the people along the way.

Through that nasty crisis I learned a lot about taking responsibility for the good and the bad that happens under my charge. The buck does stop at my desk. Whether I brought on the problem or not, the followers wanted to know what I was going to do about it. As we worked our way out of the mess I was amazed at how many people remarked that they were watching my leadership style and learned to trust and respect me for the way I handled it. Until the crisis I was somewhat of an unknown to them. But now they knew me and liked what they saw in my leadership style. I thank God for His grace in helping me survive and do a few things right in that situation!

Leaders carry the burdens of the many. Paul wrote of this in Galatians 6:2: "Carry each other's burdens, and in this way you will fulfill the law of Christ." And the apostle wrote of how God allows us to experience difficulty so that we can comfort others. "Praise be to the God and Father of our Lord Jesus Christ, the Father of compassion and the God of all comfort, who comforts us in all our troubles, so that we can comfort those in any trouble with the comfort we ourselves have received from God" (2 Cor.1:3–4).

I had that kind of an opportunity to give comfort to a group of people a few years ago. It was one of the most gripping moments of my tenure with CBInternational. Waiting impatiently at the Intercontinental Hotel in downtown Nairobi, Kenya, I didn't know whether our five missionary families in Rwanda were dead or alive. I had been scheduled to fly into Rwanda a few days earlier, but the flight was canceled when Rwanda's presidential plane was shot down and civil war erupted.

We feared for the lives of our missionaries who were in the middle of the bloodshed in the killing fields of Rwanda in 1994. Knowing that their children were on spring break and at home with their families only added to our anxiety. Normally they would have been safe at Rift Valley Academy in Kijabe, but in God's timing they were thrown into the civil war along with their parents.

I will never forget the moment at that hotel in Nairobi when I watched the United States Marine buses bring our missionaries and all their children safely into my arms. We learned that they had huddled for days in the hallways of their homes to escape machine gunfire and mortar-shell explosions. They lost everything in their homes but escaped with their lives. We are very grateful to the Belgian military and the U.S. Marines who helped them escape. Yet when they were finally safe, they were distraught over the many friends and believers they had left behind, Rwandese who were unable to be evacuated because of their nationality.

When people face intense trauma, they go through a wide range of emotions that have to be carefully worked through in the healing process. What our people needed more than anything was a heavy dose of encouragement. And for me it was an honor to be able to take them away for a week of healing, encouraging rest, and debriefing on the beaches of the Indian Ocean in Mombasa. I loved the opportunity to be able to have a direct ministry of personal encouragement in the lives of our front-line troops, a chance I rarely get because of being trapped behind my desk at headquarters. In times of crisis, leaders have a special opportunity to offer encouragement to followers that doesn't show up when all is going well.

Encourage When a Job Is Well Done

Some bosses are still hung up on the notion that it is a sign of weakness to lavish praise on their workers. Some parents still resist the notion that their children need constant encouragement as they are developing into adulthood. Both positions are fatal to healthy maturity in leadership. I have known of many hard-nosed executives who would always let people know if they stepped out of line but would never commend them when they did a job well. They are like parents who raise insecure children because they only correct them when they are wrong. Fortunately in recent years more and more management books have emphasized the need for encouragement as part of everyday leadership. Charles Schwabb believes this principle and practices it daily. He writes, "I have never seen a man who could do real work except under the stimulus of encouragement and enthusiasm and the approval of the people for whom he is working."[5]

Then there is the perspective of wisdom from seventy-five-year-old Bob Galvin (son of Motorola founder Paul Galvin) who has led Motorola through some of its greatest growth years into being one of the most successful companies in America: "It is important for leaders to spread hope, to provide the confidence level and encouragement to others in whom they have confidence."[6]

I have seen in my own organization an old attitude that still persists in some quarters—the stance that expects people to work out of a sense of duty, so why bother with praise? Christian organizations are sometimes the most guilty of this. Their reasoning goes like this: "They are working for the Lord, and He will reward them for their labors." Some even argue that it builds up egos and pride to give people praise, and therefore it is unspiritual and should be avoided.

I find that that is a pretty sad argument against lavishing your coworkers with affirmation and recognition for a job well done. Yes, I am working for that final reward from my Lord, "Well done, good and faithful servant," but I think God expects me to give affirmation as a leader along the way also.[7]

Tom Peters speaks of the need for regular encouragement. "We wildly underestimate the power of the tiniest personal touch. And of all personal touches, I find the short, handwritten nice-job note to have the highest impact . . . .

"A former boss (who's gone on to a highly successful career) religiously took about 15 minutes (max) at the end of each day, to jot a half-dozen paragraph-long notes to people who'd given him time during the day or who'd made a provocative remark at some meeting. I remember him saying that he was dumbfounded by the number of recipients who subsequently thanked him for thanking them."[8]

Along the road to effective leadership, be sure you develop the daily habit of letting people know you are pleased with them. *Become known as the pastor or boss who gives out more positives than negatives*, who is trademarked by letting people know when a job is well done.

Encourage When They Do Poorly

Good supervisors are people who, even when they must correct someone, can "step on your toes without messing up your shine." They give people a shot in the arm without letting them feel the needle. People seem to need encouragement most when they sense that they have really failed. Perhaps they failed you, failed the organization, or just failed themselves. In any case, it is at that moment that you as a leader need to show your love. If they are wounded, help them along with the healing process.

Recently Bob came into my office and unloaded a burden. He is one of the men who works directly for me. He has a lot of responsibility and quite a few people reporting to him. One of those people sent him a biting e-mail message that expressed disappointment in Bob's leadership in a particular crisis. That kind of a communiqué hurts any leader deeply. It seems that e-mail is one of the worst ways to communicate when there is conflict between people, because we fail to include the normal graces and decorum that we would include in a formal letter. We push the send button before we have a chance to see how it comes across printed out in black and white. If you are sending a heated e-mail to someone, first print it out and take the time to make sure you have said things in a fair and balanced manner with common social graces included. Hasty e-mail communiqués often make matters worse before they become better.

Bob came to me pouring his heart out about how terribly he had failed another person. I could tell he was really hurting. I have always been a firm believer in the eighty/twenty rule of success: Eighty percent of the time we will get it right, and 20 percent of the time we will blow it. So when those 20 percents come, we need to give people a lot of slack and encouragement. This is the way I operate and I expect others to do the same. I hope my board of directors gives me the same 20 percent slack I give to others.

When Bob poured his heart out to me that day, and he was beating himself up for his "blowing it" in this situation, I didn't think that what I said to him was all that profound. But he seemed to think it was. I simply told him, "Bob, I am not disappointed in you." I explained to him that we're not perfect and from time to time we make mistakes. I let him know that I had total faith in him, and I believed he was the right man for the job and that he was doing an excellent work as one of the key leaders in our organization. We thought through together how he could respond to the e-mail and rebuild the broken bridges and then he went on his way—encouraged.

Every one of us gets criticism from time to time, I explained to Bob. We learn to endure it, become wiser for it, and move on and try to make it right. For some reason, that really lifted his spirits, because I heard later that he went out of my office recovered from his disillusionment and ready to tackle the problem.

Encouragement empowers those who lead with us and provides a positive influence even when negative things are crashing around us. Because Esther had that kind of heart in the midst of crisis, she was able to be an encouragement to an entire nation. We may never be called on to save a nation as she did, but every day we as leaders are called on to be positive in a negative world.

Encourage Whenever There Is Opportunity

A new baseball coach for the Chicago White Sox was interviewed on a sports channel about how he would manage the careers of some of the multimillion-dollar players he has to coach. It is particularly difficult for a coach to lead players who make millions of dollars when the coach's salary is "only" in the six-figure category. I liked his answer: "Imposing rules without relationships incites rebellion. So my first order of the day is to get to know these guys." This coach, as the leader of some rather high-powered men, started by getting close to his team and building bridges of relationship. He will make great strides forward in that building process when times are hard. Relationships are the foundation of the encouragement process, which is such a vital part of a leader's high calling.

Paul's epistles are filled with admonitions to encourage one another whenever there is opportunity. He was a leader writing to other leaders of

Christ's church when he wrote these powerful words of encouragement to those he was leading in the faith:

> "We sent Timothy, who is our brother and God's fellow worker in spreading the gospel of Christ, to strengthen and *encourage* you in your faith." (1 Thess. 3:2)

> "Therefore *encourage one another* and build each other up, just as in fact you are doing." (5:11)

> "Preach the Word; be prepared in season and out of season; correct, rebuke and *encourage*—with great patience and careful instruction." (2 Tim. 4:2)

> "These, then, are the things you should teach. *Encourage* and rebuke with all authority." (Titus 2:15)

The writer of Hebrews also reminds us to be encouragers along the way toward maturity in the faith:

> "But *encourage one another daily*, as long as it is called Today, so that none of you may be hardened by sin's deceitfulness." (Heb. 3:13)

> "Let us not give up meeting together, as some are in the habit of doing, *but let us encourage one another*—and all the more as you see the Day approaching." (10:25)

Why is there so much about encouraging one another in the New Testament? Because by nature we are prone to discouragement. The Energizer Bunny in the TV commercial keeps showing up and going and going and going. But he has no counterpart in the real working world. Mere mortals need to have their emotional batteries charged up often.

5
CONFLICT AND CRITICISM
How to Handle Opposition

"The heart of the righteous weighs its answers, but the mouth of the wicked gushes evil." (Prov. 15:28)

ABRAHAM LINCOLN had the right idea when it came to criticism. He ignored it. "If I were to read, much less answer, all the attacks made on me, this shop might as well be closed for any other business. I do the very best I know how—the very best I can; and I mean to keep doing so until the end. If the end brings me out all right, what is said against me won't amount to anything. If the end brings me out wrong, 10,000 angels swearing I was right would make no difference."[1]

Have you ever had one of those weeks when you were criticized from every conceivable angle? It seems that every phone call brought more hurt. Then to compound the problem, it seems as if the postal service was in conspiracy with the offenders—the mail brought more misunderstandings. Not long ago I had one of those weeks. Sometimes criticisms are like blessings; they come in bunches.

When things are going well, they seem to go very well. And when they go bad, they seem to be subject to the snowball effect. How do you respond to personal attacks? How do you feel when you are misunderstood? I shut down and lose my energy and begin to stew over the cause, consequences, and cure. I suppose that some people are so thick-skinned they just grin and bear it, but most of the leaders I know take it as painfully as I do.

In that gray week I received a major personal attack from someone I thought was a good friend. In fact, as we were later debriefing the heated conflict that arose between us, he cited Proverbs 27:6, "Faithful are the wounds of a friend" (NASB). He said in effect, "As your friend I thought you wanted to hear what people are really saying." The thing that hurt me most deeply was his confirmation that he agreed with the criticism and spoke ill of me in the company of others. I am not sure those were the faithful wounds of a friend after all. One thing is for sure, he did not feel like my friend in any way that week.

Everyone in leadership faces criticism. In fact the more effective you are and the more mature you are, the more criticism you're likely to receive. Look at what happened to Paul because of his success: "A great door for effective work has opened to me, and there are many who oppose me" (1 Cor. 16:9).

Certainly the more people who follow you, the more you will be attacked. This is true because of the sheer numbers involved. If one out of ten people criticizes you and turns against you, and if you have a small following of say, ten, then you have only one to worry about. Look at what happened to Jesus, who never made a single mistake in His life! Jesus had one bad apple among His twelve. But if you are the president of the United States, one out of ten is a lot of opposition—in the millions of people! And you think you have it bad. No wonder they have entire departments at the White House just to react to criticisms.

Andrew, a friend who pastors a mid-size church in the Midwest, was discouraged and ready to look for a new job. He wrote this e-mail to me: "I have to admit today that I'm discouraged at the church situation here. I don't believe I'm getting the support I need from a couple of the deacons here, and I'm pessimistic about change. I'm writing to ask you to pray specifically that God will encourage me and show me what to do. For the first time since I've arrived here I'm seriously considering the possibility that my ministry here may be finished. If there are any church positions that you know about that may be possibilities for me or if there is a position available at CBI, I would be willing to consider them."

This is nothing unusual. In fact, I wonder how many times Andrew's thoughts are repeated all across our land each week. Gordon MacDonald says that he often thinks to himself, "Quit? Never! Run away to Switzerland and climb mountains? Every Monday!" It is not so much an issue of leaving the ministry—it's just "these particular people" and the pressure of "this situation"! A bad Sunday, a bad deacons' meeting, or a nasty letter from someone in the church criticizing you—and wham! The wind is out of your sails and the grass is looking good on the other side.

I wrote Andrew back with a few thoughts about other job possibilities, but I was sure he was just in a lull in his ministry. Sure enough, a few days later these words came to me over my data line:

> Thanks for your quick reply and for the "laughmeister" jokes. [I like to pass along e-mail humor to him; I know he needs it on Mondays!] As is usually the case, things do not look as gloomy now as they did when I wrote. However, things here in the church, especially among the leadership, seem to be going up and down. At times I just get so tired of what I would call unspiritual, nitpicky church politics which has nothing to do with the mission of the church except to detract from it. At any rate, I should know by the first of the year whether I'm really interested in making a move.
>
> A bunch of the men here went to the PK [Promise Keepers] rally in [Washington] DC and seemed to be pumped and supportive. I'm just beginning a new sermon series on repentance based on the Sermon on the Mount, entitled "What Would Jesus Say If He Lived among Us Today?" Who knows, maybe God will use all these things to unite us and get us more on track. The next two to three months will be important ones. We would appreciate the prayers of both you and Donna. Like I said, thanks so much for responding so quickly. It was encouraging just to hear from you and know that there is hope and life outside of Ourtown, USA.

I waited a few days and sent him back this reply: "Glad to hear from you, Andrew. Good to know things are on the up and up. I think we as leaders always have times when we want to give up and try fresh somewhere else, but those times usually pass. My favorite verse in those times are the profound words of the Scriptures, 'And it came to pass.' If the feelings and frustrations don't pass and things continue to go bad and burnout ensues, then I would say it is definitely time to move on."

Years ago while studying at Dallas Seminary I had the delight of having Christian psychologist Dr. Paul Meier as one of my professors for a course on Christian psychology and personality development. Much of the course was the material that became his and Frank Minirth's book, *Happiness Is a Choice*. Dr. Meier said something in class that has always stuck with me: We need to remember the eighty/twenty rule of Christian leadership. No matter what you do, 20 percent of the people may be against you just because of your personality and style of leadership. During these ensuing years of ministry I would say he is right on target. Between 10 to 20 percent of the people will be either passive and lukewarm about your leadership or downright critical. Most of them will just keep their thoughts to themselves, but every once in a while some of them will allow their criticism to perk to the surface. And there are those times when they hit you, right between the eyes, as happened to me not long ago.

BEING MISUNDERSTOOD

Have you ever been severely criticized and then written a long letter to the critic or critics? I have written my share of those letters through the years defending myself. I don't think I've actually ever mailed any of those letters, but it is a catharsis to put my emotions and thoughts on paper. If I had mailed them, I would have regretted it later after I calmed down and let reality take over.

The apostle Paul wrote one of those letters and actually mailed it. It's 2 Corinthians. One of the reasons he wrote this epistle was to answer the critics who were discrediting him before his precious Corinthian flock. Certain rival preachers had succeeded in making him look bad by distorting his motives. Look at the emotions Paul pours out in 2 Corinthians 10:9–12: "I do not want to seem to be trying to frighten you with my letters. For some say, 'His letters are weighty and forceful, but in person he is unimpressive and his speaking amounts to nothing.' Such people should realize that what we are in our letters when we are absent, we will be in our actions when we are present. We do not dare to classify or compare ourselves with some who commend themselves. When they measure themselves by themselves and compare themselves with themselves, they are not wise."

Paul went to great lengths in this letter to explain himself, rather than just defending himself. That, by the way, is a good principle when the criticism rages. It is so easy to get defensive (and we'll look at the various reactions to criticisms in a moment). But notice how Paul aggressively yet diplomatically cleared the air, point by point.

In 2 Corinthians 11, Paul wrote very intensely, defending himself from his critics. Then in chapter 12 he spoke of his vision of heaven and the thorn in the flesh God gave him. He felt foolish for his boasting: "I repeat: Let no one take me for a fool. But if you do, then receive me just as you would a fool, so that I may do a little boasting. In this self-confident boasting I am not talking as the Lord would, but as a fool" (11:16–17). "To my shame I admit that we were too weak for that! What anyone else dares to boast about—I am speaking as a fool—I also dare to boast about" (11:21). "Even if I should choose to boast, I would not be a fool, because I would be speaking the truth. But I refrain, so no one will think more of me than is warranted by what I do or say" (12:6). "I have made a fool of myself, but you drove me to it. I ought to have been commended by you, for I am not in the least inferior to the 'super-apostles,' even though I am nothing" (12:11).

Paul was torn up inside because of the misunderstandings that had been sown among his flock. As he was wrapping up the letter, he wrote, "Have you been thinking all along that we have been defending ourselves to you? We have been speaking in the sight of God as those in Christ; and everything we do, dear friends, is for your strengthening" (12:19).

Certainly it did sound like defensiveness to the Corinthians and he knew it. And yet he felt that he had to get it off his chest in the sight of God, emphasizing that all he did was out of sincere love for his dear friends, the Corinthians. It was for their strengthening that his entire ministry took place, not for his own selfish gain and for his own pride as his critics argued. No doubt Paul's words in this letter are strong. Yet we can see that he remained loyal to these believers and was totally committed to their welfare.

THE WOUNDS OF CRITICISM

Sometimes we like Paul must defend ourselves. Before we look at reasons we are attacked and how we can best respond, let's think for a moment about the damage done by criticism. During World War II the Germans waged serious warfare with one of their most potent weapons, their sleek, black underwater vessels of destruction called the U-boat (short for the German *Unterseeboot*, "Undersea boat"). These U-boats wreaked havoc in the Atlantic as the Allied forces were attempting to close in on the Germans.

When the Allied Forces detected one of these underwater warriors, they began to pummel the U-boats with depth charges and torpedoes. For days on end they would be shaken up like gravel in a cement mixer, pounded with explosives and rolling from side to side.

At times criticism can get that intense. It's been said that leaders need to have a thick skin. But that's easier said than done. I have found in my own experience that criticism cuts deeply and hurts terribly. The cute little saying that we threw around with each other as kids, "Sticks and stones may break my bones but words will never hurt me," could not be further from the truth. When we are pounded by the missiles and depth charges of friends or enemies, it does have a devastating effect on our emotions. It can bring our work to a screeching halt as we find ourselves having to deal with the criticism itself.

WHY LEADERS ARE UNDER FIRE

There are many reasons why leaders end up being attacked. At times criticism comes in the midst of a crisis, and other times it comes when things are going great. The reasons are as varied as the circumstances of leadership. Much of it has to do with the unfortunate nature of people and their selfishness, as James stated so clearly: "What causes fights and quarrels among you? Don't they come from your desires that battle within you? You want something but don't get it. You kill and covet, but you cannot have what you want. You quarrel and fight. You do not have, because you do not ask God. When you ask, you do not receive, because you ask with wrong motives, that you may spend what you get on your pleasures" (James 4:1–3).

Many times selfish motives and pride fuel conflict. The main reasons people attack others with criticism are these:

- jealousy

- unfulfilled expectations

- misunderstandings

- accurate criticisms

- organizational crisis

- values conflict

- failure

- distrust

- pride and arrogance

In response to criticism, many people react negatively. They quit, run, hide, get angry, get depressed, seek revenge, fight back, or belittle the criticizers.

TURNING THINGS AROUND

I have seen through the years that God uses criticism and personal attack to deepen and mature us. It seems to be a process that He uses to knock off the rough edges and to deepen our humility and our sense of dependence on him. In fact James wrote of this, too. "Consider it pure joy, my brothers, whenever you face trials of many kinds, because you know that the testing of your faith develops perseverance. Perseverance must finish its work so that you may be mature and complete, not lacking anything" (James 1:2–4).

When we are attacked our first response should be to realize God has something to teach us in the experience. After one particular criticism I received a number of years ago, probably one of the most painful I've ever experienced, a good friend who was mentoring me at the time said, "Hans, maybe even if 98 percent of what Jim said was wrong, there's probably 2 percent that is accurate. And that is the information God is trying to get through to you." He was right.

I had received a defamatory letter from this man I'll call Jim. His words were not the faithful wounds of a friend; they were a stab in the back from a colleague who had built a case against me over a period of several years. Why do we hide things face to face and then drop bombs with letters? In essence, he wrote me a lengthy letter, outlining point by point all the things wrong with me and why he hoped I would leave the organization. He told me this was the majority opinion of most of the people with whom I worked. To make matters worse, he waited until I was three thousand miles away to send the letter. To say the least, I was one very discouraged young servant of Jesus, questioning everything from God's goodness to my call to ministry.

For some strange reason I kept that letter, the most painful letter I have ever received. Why did I keep it in my journal? Because God used it in a powerful way to help me grow up as a leader. I pulled it out recently and read it again. And to my surprise, the pain was still very much there. Donna asked me, "Why would you pull that out and read it again? I can't believe you even kept it." After reading the letter I said, "Thank you, Lord," because I have come a long way in these twelve years in putting some of those rough edges behind me. Though the words were so painful, I thank God that he used Jim to tell me some things I really needed to hear about myself.

Today, twelve years later, I would thank Jim if I had the opportunity to see him. I did end up looking for the 2 percent and I found that it was actually more like 10 to 20 percent accurate. No matter how effective I might have thought I was, I was coming across in a way that was turning people off. I had some serious blind spots that needed correcting. Once I got over my anger and hostility toward the one who wrote the letter, the healing process began. I was on the journey toward overcoming those blind spots, and I have forgiven Jim for what he did. In fact, I'm glad he helped me see and correct some serious problems.

WHAT TO DO FIRST WHEN CRITICISM COMES

Some things we learn easily in life; others come hard. One thing we all learn sooner or later is that the first stop should be prayer. When times get tough, we must cry out to God and ask Him for His grace for the hour. God is not always ready to deliver us from conflict and crisis; that is not His way. But He does want us to ask for wisdom, understanding, and a mature response. And He can help us with our enemies, if need be. David learned to pray and seek the Lord when enemies pursued him. Here's what he wrote when his own son Absalom rebelled against him: "O LORD, how many are my foes! How many rise up against me! Many are saying of me, 'God will not deliver him.' But you are a shield around me, O LORD; you bestow glory on me and lift up my head. To the LORD I cry aloud, and he answers me from his holy hill. I lie down and sleep; I wake again, because the LORD sustains me. I will not fear the tens of thousands drawn up against me on every side. Arise, O LORD! Deliver me, O my God! Strike all my enemies on the jaw; break the teeth of the wicked. From the LORD comes deliverance. May your blessing be on your people" (Ps. 3:1–8).

Once we have voiced our concern to the Lord in prayer, we should act. Some of the best material along this line comes from Ken Williams, Wycliffe Bible Translators consultant. He has developed a list of ways to deal with personal attacks.[2] I consider these one of the greatest "finds" I've made on the subject of dealing with criticism.

Ten Biblical Ways to Diffuse an Attack

1. Keep silent (John 19:9; Prov. 17:27–28; Isa. 53:7)

2. Think before you react (Prov. 15:28; 29:20; James 1:19–20)

3. Really listen (Prov. 19:20; 18:2; James 1:19)

4. Respond gently (Prov. 15:1; 16:21; 25:15)

5. Agree (Matt. 5:25; John 18:37)

   —with whatever is true

   —in principle

   —with the possibility of truth

6. Give caring feedback (John 19:11; Prov. 15:1)

7. Ask for more (John 18:34; Matt. 5:39–41)

8. Avoid quarreling (Eph. 4:31; Prov. 17:14)

9. Offer to help (Matt. 5:40–41; Luke 6:27–28)

10. Ask for forgiveness (1 Sam. 15:24–30; 25:28)

I particularly like the final point of the list: *Ask for forgiveness.* While writing this book manuscript, I received a call from a pastor in the Midwest who had become angry with me over an issue. Thankfully this does not happen to me often! I respect this pastor for calling me. He let me know how much anger he had toward me because of my recent actions. I listened carefully and sank lower and lower in my chair. When he was finished, I was speechless. And I was at a cross-roads. The basic cause of the conflict was unfulfilled expectations; I had let him down by not doing what he expected me to do. I could have tried to explain my actions, but I realized he was right—I had failed him. So after telling him that I was guilty as charged, I asked for his forgiveness. He forgave me and we agreed to put it behind us and go on with ministry together. The wind was out of my sails the rest of that day, but I am thankful we are on the road to healing. Forgiveness was the key for our healing to begin.

BEING A REFEREE

Besides people attacking you personally in leadership, you will have times when people under your charge fight with each other. Yes, even in the church—or should we say, especially in some churches. One time two of my staff members developed such an issue between them that they refused to talk to each other. My first approach was to have an extended time with each of them to hear them out on the issue. During such a process it is imperative that you not take sides. Each knew I trusted them and understood their point of view.

Then I asked them if they could get in a room together and try to talk this thing out. I asked both of them to work more on listening to the other's point of view rather than trying to make their own points. I also encouraged both of them to eat humble pie, to be willing to ask forgiveness and admit that the problem was partially their own fault. If they had not worked it out, my next resort was to bring them in together and act as referee. But I was hoping it would not come to that. And it didn't. Later I asked one of them how it was going. "Better than ever," he replied. "We are talking with each other and listening."

When two team members can't stop fighting, here are some great guidelines from the professional world to help resolve the conflicts.

Mediate rather than judge. Tell the quarreling teammates they have to solve their problem, but let *them* decide how.

Give it time. Wait until both sides feel they've had their say and until you understand both positions before hurrying to end the conflict.

Don't accuse or lay blame. Keep everyone focused on one goal—finding a resolution. Emphasize what's right, not who's right.

Go back to basics. Focus attention on the fundamental rules, obligations, or principles in your workplace. This can help clear up fears and misconceptions that drive conflicts.

Win admissions—and forgiveness—of mistakes. Let the parties back down gracefully, and you can cut short a conflict that would otherwise last forever.

Find grounds for cooperation. Create long-term peace by crafting ways for the battling teammates to work together for mutual benefit.[3]

HAVING "THE TALK"

One way to stay ahead of an ambush—which I see happen to people from time to time—is to make it a habit to have "the talk." Recently I took the liberty of having "the talk" with my staff again. It is something I do every couple of years. What is "the talk?" It is a time when I sit down with my senior staff and tell them I want their feedback on how I am coming across as their leader. This is something I think every leader should do with the top people that surround him or her.

I do this on a regular basis with my senior staff, as well as with the chairman of my board. I don't want things to build up over a period of months or years and then one day find out, as I did in the past, that I had some major blind spots that were causing my leadership to be neutralized. I want to be vulnerable, and I want those around me to let me know if there are glaring weaknesses in my leadership.

In our organization the board chairman is my boss, as I answer to the board as my final authority. Recently he and I were having lunch and were talking about our working relationship in the coming years. At the end of the meal he asked me, "Hans, what is the best way I can help you be effective?" That was pretty easy for me. I replied, "Try to understand and support our major initiatives for ministry, and *be brutally honest with me about the job I'm doing.*"

Having "the talk" has to do with vulnerability. Bill Hybels says that people in your congregation know you have junk in your lives—they're just waiting to see if you will own up to it. That is what being open with your key staff is all about, admitting that you have junk and you want them to be part of the solution. James Emery White, a pastor in Charlotte, North Carolina, wrote about being honest with ourselves.

> Authenticity is simply being a person whose outward presentation matches reality. For pastors, that means being able to say with the apostle Paul, "We loved you so much that we were delighted to share with you not only the gospel of God but our lives as well" (1 Thess. 2:8). For too long many of us in ministry have labored under the ideal of what a pastor should look and act like. I am not saying that, in the name of authenticity, pastors should share every defeat, every failing, and every struggle without discretion. Nor should pastors parade their woundedness before the church in a maudlin sort of way. Pastors should live so our congregation knows we too are sinners.[4]

Here are some guidelines that I follow when I have "the talk." (1) Insist on personal feedback, not a ganging-up approach. One person at a time, please! (2) Limit this evaluation time to major leadership strengths and blind spots, as opposed to minor bickering and criticism. (3) Ask your staff not to discuss the session with others. (4) Keep the session verbal; don't let the staff hand you negative evaluations in writing.

Followers have always had occasions to be skeptical of their leaders. No matter how much you might respect the one in charge, you will always find certain faults that will irritate you. But when that kind of concern becomes overly critical and turns into gossip, it is unhealthy. Some churches and organizations have a cancer in their midst because it has become a serious pastime to criticize the senior pastor or leader. Some people find great joy in criticizing the sermons and actions of their leaders.

As a leader, the best thing you can do is to keep the channels of communication open by letting your leaders know you want valid criticism and feedback in the privacy of personal conversations. Hopefully that will also communicate to them that they should do likewise with their own subordinates and those who might criticize them. This spills over into annual reviews as well. Each year when I have my annual review with those people who report directly to me, I not only take the time to review their performance and contribution to the organization, but at the end of the session I ask, "How could I be a more effective leader for you? Is there anything I am doing that is making your job more difficult? Is there anything more I can do for you to help make your job more effective?"

All this is part of open and transparent communication that will keep cancerous criticism from growing to a point where it destroys your leadership and your organization's effectiveness. And don't forget to listen to what people are telling you about yourself. Follow the eighty/twenty rule, and see if 20 percent of what they are saying might have validity. Even if only 2 percent is valid, there is a message for growth in it for you.

In our organization we believe in what we call *HOT* communication: *Honest, Open,* and *Transparent.* Hopefully this helps create the type of atmosphere where we can each be a fully functioning part of the body of Christ, with respect for the role each one plays in God's grand design for our group.

> But in fact God has arranged the parts in the body, every one of them, just as he wanted them to be. If they were all one part, where would the body be? As it is, there are many parts, but one body. The eye cannot say to the hand, "I don't need you!" And the head cannot say to the feet, "I don't need you!" On the contrary, those parts of the body that seem to be weaker are indispensable, and the parts that we think are less honorable we treat with special honor. And the parts that are unpresentable are treated with special modesty, while our presentable parts need no special treatment. But God has combined the members of the body and has given greater honor to the parts that lacked it, so that there should be no division in the body, but that its parts should have equal concern for each other. If one part suffers, every part suffers with it; if one part is honored, every part

rejoices with it. Now you are the body of Christ, and each one of you is a part of it. (1 Cor.12:18–27)

Christians have a great opportunity in this arena to show the world we are different. Ever since I first read Francis Schaeffer's *The Mark of the Christian*,[5] with his challenge to believers to love each other, I have been convinced this is the key to our giving a serious witness to the unbelieving world around us. And we who are the leaders must live by positive example on the front lines of this battle.

6

VISION

Anticipating the Future

"Now faith is being sure of what we hope for and certain of what we do not see. This is what the ancients were commended for." (Heb. 11:1–2)

MARTIN LUTHER KING, JR., inspired a generation of African Americans and changed America's culture forever with his vision of a better land where freedom would reign.

These words of his challenge are well known: "I have a dream that one day this nation will rise up and live out the true meaning of this creed: We hold these truths to be self-evident: that all men are created equal. . . . When we let freedom ring, when we let it ring from every village and every hamlet, from every state and every city, we will be able to speed up that day when all of God's children, black men and white men, Jews and Gentiles, Protestants and Catholics, will be able to join hands and sing in the words of the old Negro spiritual, 'Free at last! Free at last! Thank God Almighty, we are free at last.' "[1]

King's vision of a better world did bring freedom, though it cost him his life. His vision changed the very fabric of America's culture. Though his dream is not yet fully realized, it has come a long way, and today the United States celebrates the life of this visionary leader with an annual national holiday.

Leaders are meant to be out front. They take followers to places they would not tend to go on their own. They see *farther* than others see, and they see *before* others see it. Eric Hoffer said it well: "The only way to predict the future is to have the power to shape it."[2] "The really great leaders have to be able to get ordinary people to do the extraordinary," says Wally Scott, professor of management at the J. L. Kellogg Graduate School of Management at Northwestern University.[3] But in balance we must recognize the danger of getting too far out front. I balance visionary leadership with this warning:

> **Don't be so far out in front of the troops that they mistake you for the enemy and shoot you in the back.**

Vision inspires followers. How many people choose a church because the pastor is a great administrator? I doubt any do. But if the pastor has a powerful vision for the church's ministry, people are attracted to that church. People may join a church for many other reasons, but as far as the pastor is concerned, it is his communication skills and vision, not nuts-and-bolts administration, that attracts. People care more about your leadership than your management.

The word *vision* has become one of the overused words of the nineties. I wonder how long it will last and be in vogue in our new millennium. For some of you, the very mention of "vision" is becoming as worn out as "paradigm shift." In my informal survey of various types of leaders, I find there are as many nonvisionary types as there are those we think of as entrepreneurial visionaries. For all of you who don't feel all that visionary, you probably resent the demand that vision be so important in your leadership. Hopefully this chapter will help you realize that *you do not have to be a visionary by nature to be an effective leader.*

We need to dispense with the fictitious idea that in this day of rapid change only a wild-eyed flamboyant entrepreneurial visionary can be an effective leader. Nothing could be further from the truth. Probably the best proof of the fallacy of this error is found in the book *Built to Last.* Authors James Collins and Jerry Porras dispel the myth of the visionary and instead emphasize the long-term success of *visionary companies,* or, translated into our terms, visionary churches and organizations. They studied eighteen companies that were effective for more than fifty years. Each one was led not by outstanding entrepreneurial visionaries but by leaders who were committed to building a visionary company. And all these organizations have what they call B.H.A.G's: Big Hairy Audacious Goals.[4]

The importance of vision lies *in the organization,* not necessarily in the leader. God is blessing organizations and churches today that have "big hairy audacious goals" for ministry.

Recently in Colorado Springs I sat in the office of a person who helps lead a Christian publishing company. On his wall was a large framed plaque, the centerpiece of his office decorations. The caption reads, "Attempt something so big that unless God intervenes, it is bound to fail." I like that; he knows about vision.

DAVID: MAN OF VISION

David was a man of vision. In fact the apostle Peter honored David's vision as he believed God had an incredible future in store for his nation. "Brothers, I can tell you confidently that the patriarch David died and was buried, and his tomb is here to this day. But he was a prophet and knew that God had promised him on oath that he would place one of his descendants on his throne. *Seeing what was ahead,* he spoke of the resurrection of the Christ, that he was not abandoned to the grave, nor did his body see decay" (Acts 2:29–31, italics added).

As already noted in chapters 1 and 2, David was a man of great action and character. God chose him for a lot of reasons to do His special work. And one of those reasons is that he was a man of vision.

Vision is having a clear picture of the future that a leader believes can be realized.

David developed such a picture and led his people forward toward its fulfillment.

From his earliest days it became clear that David would be a man of vision. When David was selected by Samuel to be Israel's king, the prophet "took the horn of oil and anointed him in the presence of his brothers, and from that day on the Spirit of the LORD came upon David in power" (1 Sam. 16:13). Because God's Spirit came on David, His power was demonstrated in David's life. David was protected from his enemies. David had courage and strength to fight his foes. David believed with all his heart that he and his people would be victorious.

One of the greatest displays of this power is seen when he confronted Goliath. I believe David prevailed over this giant because of David's *vision*. He believed he would prevail, and he believed that God's people were more powerful than the Philistines. Vision is like that; it can lift us up in courage to accomplish the impossible. David told Saul, "Let no one lose heart on account of this Philistine; your servant will go out and fight him" (17:32). Losing heart is what happens when there is no leadership. David believed he could prevail, but not just because he had killed a lion and a bear in the past; he believed he could defeat the uncircumcised Philistine because Goliath had "defied the armies of the living God" (17:36).

David boldly informed Goliath, "This day the LORD will hand you over to me, and I will strike you down and cut off your head. Today I will give the carcasses of the Philistine army to the birds of the air and the beast of the earth, and the whole world will know that there is a God in Israel. All those gathered here will know that it is not by sword or spear that the LORD saves; for the battle is the Lord's and he will give all of you into our hands" (17:46–47).

This attitude of faith stayed with David throughout his life. Even his years of running from Saul demonstrate that vision. Knowing he was destined for greatness, he had to wait out his time. Saul was his number-one enemy during those years of opposition. But he wasn't David's only foe. All along the journey of leadership there are those who hope you won't succeed. And the more successful you are, the more you will have your detractors. Saul's rage against David stemmed from jealousy. Because the Spirit of the Lord had departed from Saul and had moved over to David, Saul was increasingly bothered by every step of progress David made.

Eventually David became king and reigned for forty years over Israel. "David was thirty years old when he became king, and he reigned forty years. In Hebron he reigned over Judah seven years and six months, and in Jerusalem he reigned over all Israel and Judah thirty-three years" (2 Sam. 5:4–5). If David were living today, he would be considered one of the great world leaders of our time.

Though he had his deep failures as a person, David never lost the vision of what God had called him to do in serving his people. "David reigned over all Israel, doing what was just and right for all his people" (8:15). This verse underscores the fact that he was a leader who loved his people, was dedicated to them, and was their servant leader. A concluding capstone on his life is stated in Paul's reflection on David's life: "David had served God's purpose in his own generation" (Acts 13:36). For Christian leaders, that verse nicely summarizes what should be our heart's desire: to serve God's purpose in our generation.

LEADERSHIP "LIFT"

Before we look at some of the specific components of being a leader with vision, let's look at the effect of vision on followers. Men and women of great leadership ability can help lift people to great heights, a phenomenon we may call "leadership lift."

Effective leaders lift followers to heights they wouldn't normally obtain by themselves.

This is because, as stated earlier, a leader tends to see farther than others do and before others do. "A leader is one who sees more than others see, who sees farther than others see, and who sees before others do," observes Leroy Eims.[5]

For years I've had the habit of running at noontime for my own personal health and sanity. While I've lived in the Chicago area, I've managed to gather around me some colleagues who also like to run. We're known around the office as the "Run-for-lunch bunch." Three or four times a year we enjoy going out and running five-K races just to push ourselves a little harder. Some of us are fast and some of us are slow.

When I first started running regularly, I did so because the man who was my leader at that time was a jogger. I was so inspired by his life and vision that I wanted to be like him in every way. It impressed me that he had disciplined himself to take good care of his body and to run regularly. So countless times during the 1980s, as I was developing as a young leader, I enjoyed the mentorship of running along with the man I looked up to. He shared a lot of things about himself during those many runs. And he pushed me physically beyond what I thought I was capable of doing. And today as I continue to run, some of the men I run with can push me harder than I would push myself. That push, that lift, is a strong principle in leadership.

Donna and I took a radical turn in 1980 when we left a fulfilling pastorate in Southern California to pack up and move to Europe to become cross-cultural missionaries. Now twenty years later and after having watched and worked with hundreds of missionaries, I see more than ever what a tough life it is. If you stop and think of what people go through to move themselves and their families overseas to become missionaries, you might conclude they need their heads examined! They leave behind family, friends, church, employment, familiar surroundings, home, language, and the culture in which they are cozy. They usually land in a country where nothing is familiar and where the culture treats them like a body that's rejecting a transplanted organ. However, the call of God can be powerful on people's lives to cause them to implant themselves in another culture. Christ's command to "Go into all the world and make disciples" overcomes all obstacles, and so they go! Vision has a lot to do with convincing people to pack up and move overseas.

Why did our family pack up and move to another country? Why did we burn our bridges and leave behind all that was familiar? Because of vision. Particularly, because of the vision of one man: Bud Hinkson. We met Bud in the spring of 1977. He is what anyone who knew him would have to call a wild-eyed visionary. The week we met him during our last year in seminary he told me and my friends stories of God's dramatic work among the persecuted churches behind the Iron Curtain. He told of his experiences in teaching the Word of God to uneducated but eager pastors. He painted a dream, a vision, a reality far above anything we had ever imagined for ourselves. And then he challenged us to go with him. *He made the impossible seem possible.*

Bud died in a bicycle accident several years ago when he was only in his fifties. Some people would feel he didn't have enough time to accomplish all he wanted to. But Bud Hinkson leaves a legacy of hundreds of people, who, like Donna and me, left their homeland and went to another country to share the gospel and to train church leaders. Bud never went to seminary. But he made up for his lack of theological training by a deep grasp of Scripture and love for Christ. He had an *abundant dose of vision*. I have never had another experience more life-changing than the power of the vision he communicated to me.

Another reason Donna and I admired him so much was that he was a devoted husband and completely committed to his children, Jon and Joi. His wife, Shirley, continues to carry on without him, and his two children are serving the Lord as well. Though his life was consumed with ministry, it was clear to everyone that his wife and children came first. Here was a visionary who had his feet firmly planted on solid ground. Bud reminds me of the words of the Russian poet Boris Pasternak, who said, "It is not revolutions and upheavals that clear the road to new and better days, but someone's soul inspired and ablaze."

How do we go about the visioning process as leaders? Try these three steps in the process of leading your team into the future.

The Visionary Process

1. Discover the vision.
2. Dissminate the vision.
3. Drive the vision forward.

HOW TO LEAD THE VISIONING PROCESS

Discover the Vision

When the Apollo Seven astronauts left the earth in their spaceship on their voyage to the moon, they didn't aim the rocket at the moon. They aimed it at the place where the moon would be when they arrived. This is a crucial point of strategic thinking when speaking of vision; to succeed we must act in advance of the critical changes taking place in our environment.

A leader needs to consider two components of vision. One is his or her *personal vision*. This is based on your personality, gifts, experience, and passion—where you hope to be as a person. The other is your *organizational vision*, the vision of the organization you work with. Hopefully these two elements are compatible. Unfortunately, as George Barna has observed in his research, only 2 percent of pastors today can articulate their vision.[6]

The first task of the leader of a church or organization is to decide where they want to go. Where is your church heading? Have you developed a clear vision of the future and put it down on paper? Have you worked out a mission and vision statement? Do you know your leadership values?

As the leaders at CBI were developing a vision for the future of our ministry, we asked ourselves, "What do we want to look like fifteen years from now if everything goes the way we would hope it will?" This goes along with the following definition of a vision, suggested by Richard and Wendy Beckhardt: "A vision is a picture of a future state for the organization, a description of what it would like to be a number of years from now. It is a dynamic picture of the organization in the future, as seen by its leadership. It is more than a dream or set of hopes, because top management is demonstrably committed to its realization: it is a commitment."[7]

So where does this vision come from? From the leadership team—not just the one in charge. If you are a pastor, you must discover the vision for your church in concert with your leaders. Leadership is teamwork, involving the synergy of a group of people inspired by their leader. No one person has a corner on truth. I remember a frustrating time in my ministry when I was deeply troubled by what I call the apostolic style of leadership. This stands at the opposite end of the continuum from the leadership style of someone who sees his primary role as managing the resources of a team. The "apostle" views truth as coming down from on high. He knows the battle plan and where he wants the team to go. It then becomes the team's responsibility to implement the dreams and visions that are presented to them from the leader.

That approach may sound spiritual to some, but it is not biblical. The age of the apostles, when men like Peter and Paul received divine inspiration through special revelation from God, is over. The apostolic style of leadership is known in secular business as that of the visionary entrepreneur/founder who cannot let go or share ownership of the vision with others. Contrary to that, an effective leader today works *together* with his or her team to draw out ideas and organize them into clear plans and the direction in which the group will go.

> *Unless there is broad goal ownership, there will never be strong support for the leader.*

The leader must ultimately steer the group into fulfilling the mission, but defining that mission should be determined together by the organization's key players.

In our organization we rely on the guidance of God the Holy Spirit and schedule regular times of extended prayer for our leadership team. There must be serious prayer by the leadership team if we are to discover God's will in consensus. After seasons of prayer, we discuss major decisions and move ahead only if there is consensus. We rarely vote on any decisions in our ten-member executive team, for we can sense after our discussions where we stand and if there is agreement to move ahead. If one member is strongly opposed to an idea, we either drop the proposal or put it off until a later time when more information may change opinions. At times the few who may be opposed or neutral will agree to support the decision of the group for the common good.

Every organization, whether for profit or nonprofit, has a group of people with a vested interest in it. Businesses have stockholders, and churches have stakeholders. I have been working for CBInternational for almost twenty years. As a result, I have a tremendous emotional stake in our organization, a deep sense of ownership. I am not alone, of course, in that sense of ownership. As the leader, I must respect the views of the other major leaders/stakeholders in the process of developing vision for our group. I am advocating not chaos but rather orderly democracy in which key players have input and are listened to throughout the process of developing the vision. George Barna says it well: "Vision for ministry is a clear mental image of a preferable future imparted by God to His chosen *servants* and is based upon an accurate understanding of God, self, and circumstances."[8]

The key in that definition is the plural word *servants*—the leadership team. The vision must be determined by the group. A group's vision has to be somewhat dynamic and fluid in light of the times and seasons of the organization. Every few years an organization needs to reassess its vision and evaluate its impact and validity in light of current realities. "The times we are living in are much like a turbulent river," says Joel Barker. "And in times of turbulence the ability to anticipate dramatically enhances your chances of success."[9]

Disseminate the Vision

Once your leadership team has determined what your organization's vision should be, it is time to preach it from the housetops. My board of directors gave me a short list of priorities for my job, and I keep them close at hand to help me stay on target:

- Take time to pray, plan, and dream.
- Lead the staff in creative thinking.
- Be a visible communicator of the vision.
- Inspire the team.
- Inspire the constituency.

I am glad the board recognizes that vision is very much a priority in my work. "Twenty-first century leaders will lead not by the authority of their position but by their ability to articulate a vision and core values for their organizations or congregations." Thus says Aubrey Malphurs in *Planting Growing Churches for the 21*[st] *Century*. He lists seven values of understanding and disseminating your vision. He says vision provides direction, encourages unity, enhances change, allows leaders to lead, provides motivation, encourages giving, and is the basis for evaluation.[10]

I have challenged everyone in my organization to memorize our mission statement. I preach it from the housetops and print it on every brochure, flyer, and piece of literature we produce. You'll even find it on our official CBI coffee mugs! It is as important to disseminate the vision internally as it is externally.

Internal visioning is communicating to your own group what your vision and direction is. Never assume that your own people know where you are headed. Remind everyone in the system what the big picture is and where they fit in. The more they view themselves as moving the whole toward the vision, the more fulfilled they will be.

External visioning is communicating to the public and outsiders what you stand for and what you have to offer. In today's world, people respect churches and organizations that know where they are headed. Being more and more skeptical of institutions, the public demands to know why you exist and what you hope to accomplish.

Drive the Vision Forward

In a favorite "Peanuts" cartoon, Lucy asks Schroeder—who is playing the piano, of course—if he knows what love is. Schroeder stands at attention and begins to recite, "Love: a noun, referring to a deep, intense, ineffable feeling toward another person or persons." He then sits down and returns to his piano. The last panel shows Lucy looking off into the distance, saying with great disappointment, "On paper, he's great." Most vision and mission statements have the same problem: On paper they look great.

> **Your job as leader is to make the vision happen in real life in your organization, driving it forward beyond the paper.**

According to Burt Nanus, author of *Visionary Leadership,* "There is no more powerful engine driving an organization toward excellence and long-range success than an attractive, worthwhile, achievable vision for the future, widely shared."[11] Leadership must always be devoting itself to the issues of goals and strategies, asking, "Where are we going next, and why are we going there?"

Everything that happens in your church or group should be evaluated in light of that vision. Sometimes we have to give up programs that keep us too busy to accomplish the real goal. We cannot begin new initiatives that drive us to our destination if we are too busy maintaining the status quo. On the next page is a list of some enemies that work against an organization's fulfilling its stated vision.

> ### *Enemies of Vision*
>
> - *Tradition*: the way we have always done it
>
> - *Bureaucracy*: maintaining the present systems
>
> - *Inertia*: maintaining present direction
>
> - *Caution*: fear of change
>
> - *Busyness*: giving attention to urgent problems of the present instead of focusing on the future.
>
> - *Workload*: having so much to do that workers cannot dream about a better future.

Have you hammered out your corporate vision and mission? Do the troops know it? Have they memorized it? A leader's number-one job is to determine, craft, and preach the vision within and outside the organization. Based on your group's values, come up with a distinct expression of where you are going. And state that direction in a mission and vision statement.

As a leader, spend some time alone and sort out your own values for the organization. Then work it through with your leadership team and come up with a set of values and a statement of what your work is about and how you plan to accomplish it. From those core values and beliefs arise mission and vision statements that become the rallying cry of your group.

Mission and vision statements are like glue. They help leaders hold an organization together. They are like magnets, attracting newcomers as members, employees, customers, or donors. They are like yardsticks by which a leader can measure how his group is doing. And they are like a laser pointing you to your destination.[12]

During my first year as the leader of our ministry, I took our leadership team through the exercise of coming up with a fresh mission and vision statement. We went away on a retreat and determined not to come back until we had the statements hammered out. We had one requirement: No one was allowed to come to the retreat with prewritten mission and vision statements for our ministry in their hip pockets. We wanted to be sure we preserved the true "teamness" of the final results by arriving at them together.

Out of that retreat came CBI's mission and vision statements. And from those flow our nine strategic priorities as an organization. More than anything else the mission statement embodies what we, as a group, hope to accomplish. It has galvanized us in one spirit, enabling us to work toward the common goal with a renewed passion. Our mission statement is this: "In vital partnership with churches at home and abroad, the mission of CBInternational is to be a pioneering force in fulfilling Christ's Commission to the final frontiers of the harvest."

This statement has caught on well and defines our purpose. At strategic points along the way, the issues we leaders grapple with are held up to that statement and are tested by its standard. We constantly ask ourselves, "Will this help us reach our mission, or are we merely prolonging traditions which should be allowed to die a natural death?"

Stephen Covey articulates the role of leaders in finding the way for our ministries by focusing on vision. He says we must make sure we are leaning against the right wall. "We are more in need of a vision or destination and a compass (a set of principles or directions) and less in need of a road map. . . . Management is efficiency in climbing the ladder of success; leadership determines whether the ladder is leaning against the right wall."[13]

In pursuing our vision, it is important to keep the main things the main things. An effective leader must avoid getting bogged down in details and must be looking to the future. Bennis and Nanus express this point this way: "To choose a direction, a leader must first have developed a mental image of a possible and desirable future state of the organization. This image, which we call a *vision*, may be as vague as a dream or as precise as a goal or mission statement. The critical point is that a vision articulates a view of a realistic, credible, attractive future for the organization, a condition that is better in some important ways than what now exists."[14]

Isn't that what the hall of faith is all about in Hebrews 11? David and his fellow leaders of faith were honored for believing in a great future promise and hope. God was pleased with those who fought for a future that was in keeping with the good and acceptable and perfect will of God.

"Now faith is being sure of what we hope for and certain of what we do not see. This is what the ancients were commended for" (Heb. 11:1–2).

7
CHANGE

Managing Change in Your Organization

"I have become all things to all men so that by all possible means I might save some." (1 Cor. 9:22)

IF ANY ASPECT OF LEADERSHIP IS PROBLEMATIC, it is the process of introducing radical change in your organization. As early as 1532, Niccolò Machiavelli, one of the first writers on leadership, observed in *The Prince*, that "There is nothing more difficult to handle, more doubtful of success, nor more dangerous to manage, than to put oneself at the head of introducing new orders. For the introducer has all those who benefit from the old orders as enemies, and he has lukewarm defenders in all those who might benefit from the new orders."[1]

I keep that quotation on my desk as a sober reminder of what I will most likely face as a change agent. Much of leadership seems to have to do with managing change, yet nothing is more hazardous to your leadership health!

A few years ago a good friend of mine ran into a proverbial buzz saw while candidating as senior pastor. René went for the traditional week of interviews and preaching opportunities, and then had the typical open forum in which everyone in the congregation could listen to his vision and drill him with questions. He is handsome, humorous, articulate, and has great energy for ministry. He is the kind of young man many churches would love to have. This congregation would be fortunate indeed to snatch him up.

René is a man of great passion. He is also one of the best communicators I know. On the night of the open forum, he gave his impassioned presentation of the plan he would bring to this church to bring about new growth and vitality. The church had gone through several years of discouragement after the leaders had made some poor decisions. Pouring out his heart that evening, he painted a glorious picture of the future. René's vision for the church came through loud and clear. Finished with his high-energy presentation, he sat down and was ready for questions.

Immediately a hand shot up in the back of the auditorium. An elderly gentleman gave this as the first question that night: "Are you going to be walking back and forth on the platform like that every time you preach?" My friend, stunned at the level of this first question after all the passion he'd poured into his presentation, responded, "Well, uh, yes, that is my style." "Well, we don't like it!" the old man grumbled. He was reflecting not only his opinion but also that of his friends who were seated nearby. "Well, what's wrong with it, sir?" my friend asked with as much respect as he could muster. The old man answered, "We have to keep moving our heads to follow you." And you think you've got problems selling your program of change!

The end of René's story is a great one. The church did call him and he's been there several years. By the time he passed the three-year mark the church had added well over one thousand new people in weekly attendance. The last time I checked with them, he was going full blast, people were loving his ministry, and great things were happening. I guess those men got used to moving their heads back and forth!

Every pastor knows the stresses and strains involved in church ministry. It's a time of great anxiety as well as anticipation for both the congregation who is looking at the pastor and the man himself who is looking at what he got himself into. The same holds true of any leader who finds himself or herself in a new role of leadership. New leadership always brings about change, because the leader has to have the freedom to make the organization reflect its values. There is no worse situation to get yourself into than to accept a position of leadership and then be told you will not be allowed to make any changes. Avoid that situation like the plague. No matter how effective your predecessor was, you must be able to put your own imprint on the group.

WHY CHANGE?

The six last words of the church are, "We've always done it that way!" Why should churches change? Isn't the tried-and-true way good enough? Can't our ministry be successful in the future the same way it was in the past? Must big changes always be made in organizations? Can't we keep doing things the way we always have? Aren't our methods biblical? Are we just changing for the sake of change?

We've all heard these questions before. The answer: There is a vast difference between theology and methodology. Our doctrines are "given" and are permanent, but our methods must change with the times. And for those who say that is compromise, I appeal to the words of the apostle Paul, the greatest of New Testament change agents.

> Though I am free and belong to no man, I make myself a slave to everyone, to win as many as possible. To the Jews I became like a Jew, to win the Jews. To those under the law I became like one under the law (though I myself am not under the law), so as to win those under the law. To those not having the law I became like one not having the law (though I am not free from God's law but am under Christ's law), so as to win those not having the law. To the weak I became weak, to win the weak. *I have become all things to all men* so that by all possible means I might save some. I do all this for the sake of the gospel, that I may share in its blessings. (1 Cor. 9:19–23, italics added)

If you didn't know that was written by Paul, you might think the author was as spineless as a jellyfish. But Paul knew he had to adapt to different audiences with different approaches. He himself went through great changes when he shed his Pharisaical background to become an agent of the gospel to the Gentiles. Don't you think he had a lot to get over when it became clear to him that God was including the Gentiles in the gospel message?

Separating theology from methodology means seeing the difference between your group's *values* and your group's *beliefs.* Values are your "preferences," whereas beliefs are your "moral absolutes."

Contrasts between Values and Beliefs

Values	Beliefs
Preferences	Moral absolutes
Gray	Black and white
Regional/cultural	Ethical issues
Methodology	Theology
Tastes	Right and wrong

An organization's culture is the totality of how its members act, based on their values and beliefs. Here are some samples of values and beliefs. As you read the lists, answer these questions, "Which of these would I fight over? Which of these would I quit over? Which are nonnegotiable? Which do I disagree with?" Put a plus in the margin by the values and beliefs you agree with, put a minus by the ones you are neutral on, and strike out the ones you strongly oppose. When you're done, ask yourself this final question: "How many of my colleagues would answer as I did?"

Values: Preferences, tastes

- We will use the latest technology to do our work.
- More technology is better than less technology.
- Time is more valuable than money.
- The reduction of paperwork is important.
- We won't do it if it's not quality.
- Anything important will be written in a report.
- Speed is of the essence.
- Precision is of the essence.
- Our people must learn the languages in the countries where we work.

Beliefs: Moral Absolutes, Black and White Issues

- We will have open honest relationships and ask forgiveness if we wrong another worker in our organization.

- Theft will not be tolerated among our people.
- My children come before my work.
- Lying can have no place between our workers.
- We will not harbor bitterness.
- We cannot tolerate immorality among our workers.
- Planting new churches helps fulfill the Great Commission.
- We must show compassion to the poor and suffering.
- The Bible is God's inerrant, inspired revelation to humankind.
- Our workers must represent ethnic diversity.

What one person thinks is a *value* another may view as an absolute *belief.* I know Macintosh owners who are convinced it's morally responsible and imperative to be loyal to Apple!

To some people the world is black and white, and everything is a moral issue. They cannot see shades of gray; they tend to be rigid thinkers. I find such people are hard to work with and hard to work for. They tend to see the world in rigid categories and to think that their way is the only way.

It is extremely important to distinguish between values and beliefs. Every issue is not worth fighting over, and many times we have to respect the rights of others who have a different set of values or beliefs.

As a leader, spend some time alone with yourself and sort out your own set of values and beliefs. Then work with your leadership team and come up with a list of values and beliefs your team stands for. These two lists can become a powerful glue holding you together like layers on a sheet of plywood.[2]

As a shepherd/leader, you are responsible to help your congregation or group face the future with both eyes open, to help them face change head on.

Why change? A number of reasons impel us to make our churches flexible in a changing environment. Some of the top reasons are these:

1. *God is stirring our hearts to do a new thing.* Often as a result of serious prayer, God the Holy Spirit stirs the hearts of leaders to start afresh and do a new thing in their ministries. And leaders beware—sometimes the stirrings begin at the bottom of the organizational chart!

2. *A growing sense of urgency.* At times you may sense a complacency in ministry, and God will give you a new sense of urgency to rekindle your first love and foremost priorities.

3. *The changing nature of our audiences.* The people to whom we are called to minister are changing dramatically today.

4. *The changing nature of our workers.* With the arrival of Generation X into our mainstream work force, new demands are being made on managers of workers and volunteers.

5. *Demographics.* Your community and social surroundings have changed *dramatically.* Have you changed with it?

6. *Changing markets and ministries.* The way you carry out your ministry may need to be changed in light of external changes.

7. *Lack of organizational vision.* Are you suffering organizational *poor blood?* Is there lack of passion in your ministry? Is there chronic organizational drift?

8. *Organizational ineffectiveness.* Are you no longer effective in what you are in service to accomplish?

9. *Patterns of repeated failure.* Are you seeing one failure after another in your programs?

10. *Lack of clear goals and objectives.* Does everyone have a different version of where you should be going and what your priorities are?

11. *Plateaued ministry.* Is nothing exciting happening in your church or group—just more of the same as last year?

12. *Decline in impact.* Along with internal failure and drift, is there an obvious lack of visible, viable results?

13. *High attrition levels.* Are people not attracted to your group?

14. *Confusion about lines of responsibility/authority.* No one seems to know who is actually responsible for what, so there is considerable wasted effort, confusion, and poor use of resources.

15. *Low morale.* People are discouraged about being members of your staff. Faithful insiders are hanging on out of sheer loyalty, not because of heartfelt passion for the work.

16. *Ongoing financial failure.* You end every year in the red. Or you are in the black only because of those godly people who bequeathed their estates to your ministry.

No doubt other reasons could be given on why we make changes. But this list is a start in facing the mountain of challenge that lies before us. And we leaders are the ones to be most concerned about doing something about what we see. Followers may see the problems, but they will wait for us to take the risks to bring about change. Regardless of how your group got there and what the growth needs are, the leaders must be the chief pioneers for the change process. Kouzes and Posner put it like this: "Leaders are pioneers. They are people who venture into unexplored territory. They guide us to new and often unfamiliar destinations. People who take the lead are the foot soldiers in the campaigns for change . . . the unique reason for having leaders—their differentiating function—is to move us forward. Leaders get us going someplace."[3]

FROM LEMONS TO LEMONADE

The Old Testament records the story of a young man who was thrown into a life of change when he was a teenager.

Joseph was forced by life's circumstances to be an agent of change. When life kept throwing him one lemon after another, he became an expert in the lemonade business. I doubt there is any other person in the Bible who had to recover from so many upheavals. The great lesson is that Joseph always came out on top.

Stephen summarized what was dealt to Joseph and how he responded.

Because the patriarchs were jealous of Joseph, they sold him as a slave into Egypt. But God was with him and rescued him from all his troubles. He gave Joseph wisdom and enabled him to gain the good will of Pharaoh king of Egypt; so he made him ruler over Egypt and all his palace.

Then a famine struck all Egypt and Canaan, bringing great suffering, and our fathers could not find food. When Jacob heard that there was grain in Egypt, he sent our fathers on their first visit. On their second visit, Joseph told his brothers who he was, and Pharaoh learned about Joseph's family. After this, Joseph sent for his father Jacob and his whole family, seventy-five in all.

Then Jacob went down to Egypt, where he and our fathers died. Their bodies were brought back to Shechem and placed in the tomb that Abraham had bought from the sons of Hamor at Shechem for a certain sum of money.

As the time drew near for God to fulfill his promise to Abraham, the number of our people in Egypt greatly increased. Then another king, who knew nothing about Joseph, became ruler of Egypt. (Acts 7: 9–18)

This excerpt from Stephen's speech to the Sanhedrin clearly portrays the groundwork of God's providential working through young Joseph. God was going to send his people to Egypt for a four-hundred-year exile. Stephen said, "God spoke to [Abraham] in this way: 'Your descendants will be strangers in a country not their own, and they will be enslaved and mistreated four hundred years. But I will punish the nation they serve as slaves,' God said, 'and afterward they will come out of that country and worship me in this place'" (7:6–7).

Joseph had little idea he would be the major player God would use to pave the way for the Israelites to be in Egypt for four centuries. During those years they would be protected from famine and possible extinction in their homeland of Canaan, and God would accomplish His purposes with the pagans in that part of the world. As Joseph's brothers all eventually settled in Egypt, the Israelites had the opportunity to grow under Joseph's political protection. Then one day Moses would lead them out of Egypt.

As a change agent Joseph was a man with big dreams (a vision). Having vision is a prerequisite characteristic of anyone with a serious change agenda. If there are no big dreams for change, then why not leave things the way they are? In Joseph's case God was working behind the scenes to protect His people; He needed Joseph out front to be the main agent in that plan. Perhaps Joseph's flexibility was his greatest asset, since the more life threw at him the stronger he became in the midst of change. Though many of us naturally fear change, it can be our friend and make us stronger.

In his young life Joseph got off to a difficult start. His father Israel "loved Joseph more than any of his other sons because he had been born to him in his old age" (Gen. 37:3). When his brothers saw that their father loved him more than any of them, they hated him and "could not speak a kind word to him" (37:4). Besides being favored by his father, Joseph also had dreams that drove his siblings to hate him. Joseph was a dreamer, and it turned out in the end that God had given him these dreams as a vision of what would be in the future.

Joseph was not perfect, and one of the mistakes he made as a visionary dreamer was to be less than tactful and diplomatic in his presentation of his dreams to his brothers. If you have great plans for your people, be careful how they are delivered! The younger you are the more careful you need to be. From what we read in Genesis 37, apparently he must have displayed a spirit of arrogance as he told his brothers he would end up ruling them.

Not everyone will be sold on the dreams of a change agent. In fact, experience shows that most people will be lukewarm or negative rather than positive toward new ideas. Certainly Joseph's brothers had no desire to see his dreams realized, so they set out on their plot to kill him. "So Joseph went after his brothers and found them near Dothan. But they saw him in the distance, and before he reached them, they plotted to kill him. 'Here comes that dreamer!' they said to each other. 'Come now, let's kill him and throw him into one of these cisterns and say that a ferocious animal devoured him. Then we'll see what comes of his dreams'" (37:17–20).

And you think you've had opposition to *your* dreams? At each step of the way, Joseph found resistance but responded with a change agenda that eventually accomplished God's purposes for his life and for his followers. Let's look at some of the problems Joseph faced and how he responded.

1. *Abandoned*: He was thrown into a well by his brothers, then pulled back out of the well and sold into slavery. What did Joseph think about during the hours he lay in that well? He probably believed it wasn't the end for him. He really believed in the dreams he had and that God had a great future for him. So presumably either he was waiting for his brothers to leave so he could figure how to get out, or he was waiting for someone to lift him out.

2. *Betrayed*: He was sold as a slave by his brothers to the Ishmaelites.

We read nothing about Joseph's response during the time he was in the hands of the Ishmaelites. We can only assume that he had the same attitude he did at the bottom of the well. Things seemed to be getting worse, but perhaps this was a way for things to get better. Maybe he took a wait-and-see attitude, not even knowing where he was heading.

3. *Transplanted culturally and socioeconomically:* Joseph was made a slave in Potiphar's household. He definitely had a good attitude because he immediately went to work and soon prospered. Genesis 39:2–4 reads, "The LORD was with Joseph and he prospered, and he lived in the house of the Egyptian master. When his master saw that the LORD was with him and that the LORD gave him success in everything he did, Joseph found favor in his eyes and became his attendant." This does not sound like the kind of person who was only trying to get back home to his family. No, he was responding to the change that was being thrown at him and he was making the best of a bad situation.

4. *Tempted:* Potiphar's wife attempted to get Joseph to sleep with her. No matter what the temptation, Joseph held his ground. "And though she [Potiphar's wife] spoke to Joseph day after day, he refused to go to bed with her or even be with her" (39:10). Can you imagine the kind of temptation he was under? He was "well-built and handsome" (39:6), and no doubt Potiphar's wife was attractive. She took notice of Joseph and constantly begged him to go to bed with her. No doubt they were alone many hours in the house each day, time that gave opportunity for compromise. But he stood his ground and kept his character intact.

5. *Framed and imprisoned:* Joseph was thrown into prison when Potiphar's wife falsely accused him of attempted rape. Joseph again made lemonade from the lemons thrown his way. But "the LORD was with him; he showed him kindness and granted him favor in the eyes of the prison warden. So the warden put Joseph in charge of all those held in the prison, and he was made responsible for all that was done there. The warden paid no attention to anything under Joseph's care, because the LORD was with Joseph and gave him success in whatever he did" (39:21–23).

6. *Faced a national crisis:* Joseph was called on to interpret Pharaoh's dreams. Pharaoh had searched his kingdom to find someone to explain the meaning of his dreams. God arranged for Joseph to have an audience

with Pharaoh to interpret the dreams. Pharaoh immediately saw that Joseph's dream interpretation was correct and obviously was from God. Joseph gave the credit to God, and recommended a radical change in the normal way of managing crops in Egypt! At the age of thirty, Joseph, fresh from prison, found credibility with Pharaoh. He was immediately appointed second in command over all Egypt, in charge of collecting grain for the protection of Egypt from the coming famine (41:39–57).

7. *Shed bitterness and showed forgiveness*: Joseph was finally reunited with the brothers who sold him into slavery when they came to Egypt for food. Even though bitterness and resentment could have built up in his heart, he treated his brothers with great love and kindness. Why? Because he understood that what had happened to him was part of God's plan. The fact that Joseph was not made bitter by the difficulties he faced was one of the keys to his success.

8. *Preserved the nation*: He saved his family from famine. When Joseph's father, Jacob, and his entire family moved to Egypt, Joseph went to Pharaoh to request help in relocating his family. Pharaoh respected Joseph so deeply that he eagerly accepted his family into Egypt. Pharaoh gave the Israelites the best land in all Egypt for their crops and homes! He even gave them employment by hiring them to tend his flocks (47:1–7).

Joseph's life can be summarized by his statement to his brothers, "You intended to harm me, but God intended it for good to accomplish what is now being done, the saving of many lives" (50:20).

Joseph was an adapter—and also a thriver. He knew how to make the best of his circumstances, whether in a palace or a prison. When dramatic changes came his way, he creatively coped with each new situation. He even mastered life in a foreign culture far from his homeland, becoming part of the king's household and "prime minister" of his adopted land. How can we summarize the lessons learned from the life of Joseph in the process of change? Several principles are evident in Joseph's life of change.

JOSEPH: CHANGE AGENT

- *Vision:* He kept his dream alive.
- *Determination:* He expected opposition.

- *Flexibility:* He improvised.
- *Diplomacy:* He made enemies his allies.
- *Creativity:* He used what was available.
- *Character:* He resisted temptation.
- *Endurance:* He never lost faith.
- *Positive outlook:* He looked for the silver lining.
- *Humble dependence:* He knew God had a plan and would open the way.

THEY CHANGED THE RULES!

The problem with the *Titanic* was not only Captain Smith. The rudder was also to blame; it was too small. Once the men on the lookout deck spotted the iceberg, First Officer Murdoch tried to turn the giant vessel out of harm's way. As the ship was sinking, even the builder admitted that the rudder was not large enough. Many organizations have failed because they were not equipped to change fast enough to deal with crises. The groups we lead into this next century must have a built-in flexibility that will enable them to respond to the rapid pace of external change.

Futurist Alvin Toffler observes, "The illiterate of the 21st century will not be those who cannot read and write, but those who cannot learn, unlearn, and relearn." Two recent incidents underscored for me how the world today differs dramatically from the world I grew up in the fifties and sixties. One had to do with my own teenage son and the other with some Generation Xers who work in our organization.

On a Wednesday night I was picking up Mark from his youth group, "The Cause." As I sat in the parking lot with the car window open, I couldn't help but hear the teenagers talking with each other. My son walked out and instead of coming over to my car, he went over to a group of his friends. Mark had just bought his first personal computer with his own money. His friends began to ask him questions about how much RAM it had, what kind of video cards it had, how many gigabytes the hard drive had, what kind of resolution was on the monitor, and how fast his CD-ROM was.

As they were bantering about in the parking lot, bragging about the size of "the RAM under the hood," I laughed as I flashed back thirty years to when I was standing around in the parking lot of my old high school. Back then we would brag to each other about the size of the carburetor under the hood of our cars. We would get our hands greasy and grimy trying to tune up our street rods and were well versed in things like carburetors, pistons, rods, torque, and the like. Bragging rights were reserved for how many seconds it would take to get up to sixty miles per hour, whereas Mark bragged to his friends about the speed of his video drivers on his new PC system.

The second event that awakened me to the different world of the next generation happened by e-mail recently. I received a communiqué, from one of our new Generation-X couples based in West Africa. After discussing our orientation program, they reflected on the type of organization to which they want to be loyal for the long haul. They wrote, "We're not bound by what's been done in the past; we prefer to develop our own solutions to age-old problems. Tell us the story of the past problem and how the solution was arrived at, but don't labor us with burdens of rules from past problems. We want a chance to solve the problem in a new, contemporary, yet thoroughly biblical way."

Chapter 8 includes a list of characteristics of this new generation. I am high on Generation X, but I know they will need to be led differently than people in previous generations. And that calls for change.

Each generation has its own values and culture based on what life was like during their formative years before they reached age twenty. If you are older, just compare the world as it was when you were a teenager to the life of teenagers today. The teens of the eighties and nineties are our work force of tomorrow. They will fill our churches and work in our organizations and are wired in ways we must come to understand.

CHANGE IS THE ONLY CONSTANT

As a servant leader, one of the most valuable contributions you can make is to help your church or group adjust to the realities of today's ministry climate. Organizations of the future must be flexible, adaptive, and quick in response. Pastors and other Christian organizations must respond to new challenges, just as business organizations have learned to interact with an extremely competitive environment. Christian leaders out of touch with fast-paced changes may find their ministries becoming obsolete. When I was asked to become the CEO of our ministry, the board asked me if I had any fears. Without hesitation, I answered, "My greatest fear is that CBInternational will become irrelevant." What good is it if we continue to exist but are marginalized?

Unless we are responsive to change as organizations, we may soon become extinct.

Whether you are leading a church, a business, a parachurch ministry, or other organization, you must be a change agent. This comes with the job. So how do we learn to be effective change agents? There are a number of ways, one of which is to read as much as you can about what is happening in the world in which you work, the industry in which you serve, and society in general. It is also important to read books written by great leaders who are uniquely gifted to speak to other leaders.

Several years ago Leith Anderson spoke in a seminary chapel on the topic "Ministry, Not the Same Yesterday, Today, and Forever." In this address he spoke of ten trends in ministry today that differ significantly from values in former decades.

1. Yesterday, faithfulness was good enough. Today, faithfulness is not good enough; you also need effectiveness.
2. Yesterday, godliness was assumed but not required. Today, godliness is required but not assumed.
3. Yesterday, pastors had been prepared and trained. Today, they have to be lifelong learners.
4. Yesterday, reason was more important than relationship. Today, relationship is more important than reason. Today, more than ever before people are drawn into a church because of a relationship within small groups and programs as opposed to listening to reasoned sermons in large sanctuary settings.
5. Yesterday, pastors had less to read. Today, there is more information available for pastors, perhaps more than they can assimilate. Some may even be worn out by the information explosion.
6. Yesterday, the center of influence was denominations and semi-

naries. Today, the center of influence is megachurches and seminars. Megachurches have been a great threat to seminary professors and denominational leaders. But, we must face the fact that megachurches are influential, and they have the ability to read culture and know how to relate to it. That's where megachurches excel.

7. Yesterday, preaching was more important than programs. Today, programs are more important than preaching. Large churches are no longer built on a strong pulpit ministry alone.

8. Yesterday, ministry depended on a leader. Today, ministry depends on a team. Hierarchy is dead and self-directed ministry teams are the order of the day. Back in the sixties, medical TV shows included *Marcus Welby, M. D.*; *Dr. Kildare;* and *Ben Casey.* Today the hot medical programs are all related to teams: *ER* and *Chicago Hope.*

9. Yesterday, success was defined by narrow comparison. Today, success is defined by a wide comparison. Yesterday a pastor's ministry was compared to that of the prior pastor or other pastors in a given community. Today, comparisons are made all across the country because of the mobility of people and the explosion of access to information.

10. Yesterday, pastors spoke more about families and marriage. Today, there is less said about family and marriage because the clergy feel discredited as a result of personal crises. Pastors tend to keep quiet because divorce and disasters happen to them and to their families, too.[4]

HOW TO IMPLEMENT CHANGE

A few months ago I dropped a "change bomb" on our office staff. Our board of directors had decided it was time to move our ministry headquarters from Wheaton, Illinois, to Denver. For a ministry located for fifty-five years in the Midwest with forty of those years in the same building, that was a big announcement. Relocations can be very unsettling, and I knew that the announcement would send shock waves through the system. When the dust settled and the troops heard what was up, they warmed up quite well to the idea.

Perhaps the greatest reason we were successful in launching this change process is that we carefully worked through the circles of ownership of the change over a period of months. By the time the decision was announced publicly, there was already maximum ownership and minimum resistance.

Bringing about change in an organization involves taking information through circles of stakeholders, working from the inside out.

The more bases you cover before the change is made public, the better your chances for positive ownership of the idea. A few people will be upset that they were not "in the know," but most people will back your program. If there is major opposition, you will have already encountered it during the process of moving outward with the information.

Picture six circles, each inside the other. The circle in the center is the board, and the next circles, moving toward the outside, are your leadership team, the close general management circle, key stakeholders, those who may be anticipated opponents, and the general members of the organization.

Recently someone asked executive consultant Stephen Covey if it is possible for a chief executive officer to change culture, or if he or she must simply adapt to the culture. He answered this way: "I think both. He has to adapt in the sense that he deals with where the culture is now. And therefore he cannot just artificially and unilaterally impose a whole new system and a bunch of new guidelines. But a CEO also has a vision and a mandate . . . to make some fundamental changes that, deep inside the bowels of the organization, people have known for a long time should take place. . . . A CEO also should respect that you don't announce a culture, you don't mandate it, you don't legislate it. It happens naturally inside the hearts and minds of people."[5]

Then he was asked, "What separates CEOs who fail from those who succeed?" His answer makes a lot of sense. "They don't know how to bring about a change in the culture. You see, business basically is run by the economic rules of the marketplace, but organizations are run by the cultural rules of the workplace. They are not in alignment. A lot of people over time have become dependent on the old cultures and systems, and it takes a lot of courage to change the structures and systems."[6]

Changing the culture, structure, and systems is indeed a delicate process. Here are some of the reasons people do not want to change.

Reasons Why Followers Resist Change

1. *Fear:* The unknown is a threat to people's comfort zones.

2. *Insecurity:* People may think they will be worse off after the changes.

3. *Power:* People sense the change may cause them to lose power.

4. *Inertia:* It is easier to maintain the status quo.

5. *Energy:* It takes a lot of work to change things.

Change will have many detractors. It is up to the leaders to champion the cause with careful planning and a solid rationale. When implementing major change in your church or organization, try to follow these eight steps carefully:

EIGHT STEPS TO EFFECTIVE CHANGE

First, prepare carefully. The more carefully you have done your homework the easier it will be to sell your ideas. If you can explain the changes in a convincing manner, you will get maximum ownership. If your reasons lack credibility, don't bother going on to the other steps.

Second, learn from the past. Don't just change for the sake of change. Learn what in the past should be preserved and find out if your predecessors wrestled with the same issues. Why did they decide to do things this way?

Third, gain ownership from the inside out. Follow the circles of ownership discussed earlier. Make sure the greatest number of people possible can be lined up on your side of the change process. The fewer the resisters, the better the chances of success.

Fourth, count the cost. Will you truly be better off doing it the new way? Is the juice worth the squeeze? Have you calculated what emotional and physical toll the changes will take on you and your organization?

Fifth, anticipate resistance. Determine what individuals and groups may oppose your proposal. What can you do to bring them along and make them your allies?

Sixth, listen and learn. Two of the most important words in any leader's vocabulary should be *listen* and *learn*. Listening means you respect your followers and welcome their input. By the time the change process is complete, all stakeholders should have their fingerprints on the outgrowth.

Seventh, use experts. Don't reinvent the wheel. Learn from others who have gone before you in the change process. Use consultants and outside experts to strengthen your hand. The more data you have to support your decisions, the more effective will be their positive effect on the organization.

Eighth, take your time. Rushed decisions follow the old pattern of "ready, aim, fire." It is better to let the process of change take a slower, more natural course, which will gain more support over the long haul.

How do your members react when change comes? What is their first response when the bombs are dropped? Responses vary from person to person. When we announced our decision to move to Denver, one of my young Generation X employees was gleeful. "I think it is so cool that everything is up for grabs. Nothing like radical change to make work a fun place!" Other longtime employees were not so positive and burst into tears of grief and fear.

It is natural to face resistance in the change process. Employees and followers will go through five phases in their processing of major changes in churches and organizations.

Reactions of Followers to News of Change

1. *Denial:* Withdrawal, focusing on the past.
2. *Resistance:* Anger, blame, anxiety, depression, apathy.
3. *Exploration:* Concern about details, confusion, energy, new ideas, lack of focus.

4. *Commitment:* Cooperation, better focus, anticipation of the challenges ahead.
5. *Rejection:* Some will move on to other places.

It is normal in the process of change to lose some people. We should expect it and not be alarmed. In some cases losing people is a good thing as some habitual resisters are thinned out of the ranks. If we lose a large number, then things are probably not going as they should.

TRANSFORMATIONAL LEADERS

When you find yourself in need of bringing about major changes, you have the choice to go fast or slow. Usually the best approach is to take your time. Recently Bruce, a friend of mine from the East, moved from a pastorate in New York City to Portland, Oregon. This brother is a street-wise New Yorker who knew he was making a huge cultural jump to pastor a suburban congregation in Portland. Having just completed his first year in the new pastorate, he is beginning to implement bold change.

I like Bruce's process as a transformational leader. He told me he carefully followed the principle of not making any changes the first year. He spent a lot of time listening and a lot of time talking to the congregation. In fact, one of the smartest things he did was to take the time to visit all the elderly of the congregation in their homes. Many of them were amazed; this had never happened to them before. During this first year as he met the people in their homes and built coalitions of loyalty, he won friends and influenced a lot of people. Today he has the congregation ready to jump wherever he wants to take them.

What Bruce did is what experts tell us we should all do. Stephen Covey, whose leadership development company, Franklin Covey, consults with some of the leading companies of the world, shares these words of wisdom for new leaders coming in from the outside who are expected to turn around an organization (or a church):

I would first of all say that they have two ears and one mouth and they should use them accordingly.

They should listen a lot before they speak and before they attempt to synergize with the group. Otherwise they can make all the commitments they want to the shareholders and to the public, but if you don't get cultural support then, there will be disillusionment downstream later on.

And the more they listen and involve people in identifying the present reality that they're in and some of the goals that are being proposed, as well as the reason they have been brought in . . . then they can begin to deal with the issues of how you can go from here.

The more people feel involved in that problem, the more they'll be part of the solution. But if they're not involved in the problem and they're just kind of arbitrarily and unilaterally informed and then these new goals are announced, you could have enormous cultural resistance and they won't become an agent of change.[7]

I can't help but think that Joseph followed this approach in all the changes he faced. He may have made friends with the slaveowners who first bought him; then he got to know the workers in Potiphar's household. Everywhere he went he listened and won respect. If Joseph were alive today, we would say he had masterful people skills. He gained influence and position because God blessed him and because he knew how to make his allies stronger. Even in prison he became chief in command!

What does all this mean? It means we can't have change and maintain the status quo at the same time. We can't be heavily engaged in maintaining the present status while giving ourselves aggressively to new visions and initiatives. Something has to go in order for the future to come. We must become proactive transformational leaders.

We cannot simply be responders; we must actively pursue a course that will successfully guide our group into the future. Phillip Lewis summarizes the characteristics of a leader who succeeds as a change agent in God's work.

Transformational Leaders

- Are open to God's transformational work in their lives, so they may, in turn, transform others, leading people to a closer, more intimate relationship with Jesus Christ.

- Change markedly, and for the better, the people and organizations with which they work.

- Inspire others to excel, giving people individual consideration and stimulating them to think in new ways.

- Increase their ability to lead by being fair, developing credibility, building morale, and communicating respect.

- Strengthen their legitimate power base through consistency, gentleness, kindness, openness, and patience.

- Start building today what will be needed in the kingdom tomorrow.

- Focus on what to do next, realizing organizational development is never-ending.

- Recognize the telltale signs of decline and, when needed, they regroup, replan, restructure, and rethink.

- Create a vigorous relationship between leaders and followers.

- Excel at communicating ideas, motivating people, and understanding what others are saying and thinking.

- Employ a rational approach toward anticipating, responding to, and altering the future.

- Are innovative, willing to begin again, creative, always introducing something new.

- Question every program that uses time, energy, and money.

- Create a compelling picture of the future.

- Have faith in their dream, their abilities, and God's power in them to bring those dreams into reality.

- Are willing to dream impossible dreams.

- Understand their opportunities and threats, and can identify where they can be most effective.

- Are open with their followers, keeping them informed of what is happening.

- Know how to give and receive constructive criticism by placing a high priority on understanding.

- Are able to look inward, analyzing whether they are promoting effective growth or hindering excellence.[8]

Sometimes leaders in ministry succeed, and other times they fail. Why is it that some leaders can go into a new situation and completely turn it around, whereas someone else may go into that same situation and fail? I have seen friends resign from a situation out of discouragement, having given up the change process. It is difficult to discern whether the problem was with the person, the followers, or the situation. Sometimes it is the fault of the people being led. But often it is a stumbling along the way in the process of change for all parties involved: the leader, the leadership team, and the people.

Change, as Machiavelli said five centuries ago, is "difficult to handle."[9] The more we learn to master the process and deal with it cautiously, the more likely we are to succeed as effective leaders of change agents.

8

THE LEADERSHIP TEAM

Developing the Leaders Around You

"Whatever you have learned or received or heard from
me, or seen in me—put it into practice. And the God of
peace will be with you." (Phil. 4:9)

THEODORE ROOSEVELT said, "The best executive is the one who has
sense enough to pick good men to do what he wants done, and self-
restraint enough to keep from meddling with them while they do it."[1] Although team leadership is not quite that simple, Roosevelt was on the right
track with these words. There is no substitute for having all the right people
on your ministry team. They will make or break your effectiveness as a leader.

**Your leadership effectiveness rises or falls by the people who
surround you.**

An angry Doberman near our office illustrates a valuable lesson about
mentoring. My twenty-year habit of running at noontime is a great way to
break up the fatigue of working at a desk job. Not far from our office is a
beautiful forest preserve and nature trail where running is refreshing,
whether in the heat of summer or in a foot of snow. On the way to our
running path, our "Run-for-lunch bunch" passes a fenced-in yard, where
there is a large Doberman. As we run by, his fierce barking grows to a fe-
vered pitch as he paces the fence and jumps vertically in a vain attempt to
get at us by clearing the fence. Half of his body actually does rise above the
top of the fence, but he always returns to the ground with a disappointed

thud. The thought of us being attacked by this dog is unsettling, but we have grown accustomed to the knowledge that he will never reach his potential. In fact lately we have been egging him on with encouragement to try harder. We've even been barking back!

What amazes us each time we run by this dog is that the fence is actually quite low and he is considerably large; he doesn't know he could easily clear the fence with a running jump. Here is this powerful dog with the potential to easily get to his objective—us—but he has never been mentored in the fine art of jumping fences. Hopefully the owners will never get another dog that could teach him! Each time I run by that dog he reminds me of one of my responsibilities as a leader: Help people reach their potential to jump over the barriers in life they think are insurmountable. Like this dog, many people under our charge have self-imposed limits from which we must free them. Leaders need to show them how they can stretch above their limitations and reach their potential. Warren Bennis observes, "The successful leader of tomorrow will not have the loudest voice, but the readiest ear. His or her real genius may well lie not in personal achievement, but in unleashing other people's talent."[2]

That is the essence of mentoring a leadership team: a relational experience in which one person empowers others by sharing God-given resources. Bobby Clinton defines mentoring more formally: "A mentor is a person with a serving, giving, encouraging attitude who sees leadership potential in a younger leader and is able to promote or otherwise significantly influence that younger leader along to the realization of his/her leadership potential."[3]

Any leader's first task is to build the leadership team. Yet finding the right leaders can be your greatest challenge. Do you have a good leadership pool in your church to draw from? Is your organization blessed with talent that can be tapped? Whenever possible, it is better to promote from within rather than going outside for new leadership. If good people are passed over on the inside, the message they get is that they are not valued and that there is no potential for their career growth. In fact passing up qualified insiders for what appear to be more talented outsiders can hurt the organization in more ways that one. Short-term gains may be achieved at the expense of diminishing long-term loyalty among the majority.

When I stepped into the leadership of CBI, most of the senior people were retiring. Though the old team was a great team, it was time for fresh leadership with new people. I was able to select a fine group of men and women who share the vision and values I feel are critical. We have the great foundation of our predecessors to build on, yet the freedom to move ahead into a new day of ministry.

Experts today say we are moving into an era when individual leadership is being replaced with group leadership. According to Max DePree, "The measure of leadership is not the quality of the head but the tone of the body. The signs of outstanding leadership appear primarily among the followers."[4] This idea of laying aside egos for the good of the team was a biblical idea long before it became popular in present-day management. Paul spoke of laying aside our egos for the sake of the whole. "If you have any encouragement from being united with Christ, if any comfort from his love, if any fellowship with the Spirit, if any tenderness and compassion, then make my joy complete by being like-minded, having the same love, being one in spirit and purpose. Do nothing out of selfish ambition or vain conceit, but in humility consider others better than yourselves. Each of you should look not only to your own interests, but also to the interests of others. Your attitude should be the same as that of Christ Jesus" (Phil. 2:1–5).

One of the top experts on leadership today is Warren Bennis, distinguished professor of business administration at the University of Southern California. He teaches in the classroom, writes prolifically, and is a consultant to multinational companies and governments throughout the world. In a recent article he wrote about the fact that great groups make strong leadership teams. "Great Groups make strong leaders. On the one hand, they're all non-hierarchical, open, and very egalitarian. Yet they all have strong leaders. That's the paradox of group leadership. You cannot have a great leader without a Great Group and vice versa. Great Groups are the product of meticulous recruiting. Cherry-picking the right talent for a group means knowing what you need and being able to spot it in others. It also means understanding the chemistry of a group."[5]

In picking your team, pass your present leaders and any potential future leaders through a carefully thought-out leadership recruitment grid.

An extremely important task of a senior pastor or ministry executive is to pick the right team to surround him. In interviewing potential leadership staff, I ask and look for answers to the following questions.

LEADERSHIP TEAM INTERVIEW QUESTIONS

1. *Do you share a passion for our mission statement?* Are we headed in the same direction? Do you understand our mission and vision, and do you buy into it with your whole heart?
2. *Are we doctrinally on the same page?* If you do not share the same biblical convictions, you will have trouble as a team.
3. *Are you committed to growth?* Is growth a high value for you? Are you open to abandoning the status quo, when necessary?
4. *Do you complement the team with your gifts?* Can your natural abilities and spiritual gifts make a unique contribution to the team?
5. *Will you be a team player?* What do you understand to be the meaning of the word *team*? Are you a loner, or are you committed to being a part of the community of leadership?
6. *Do you hold to our leadership code of conduct?* How do your values and convictions compare with those of our organization?
7. *Do you get along well with people?* What conflicts have you faced with others, and how were they resolved?
8. *Are you fun to work with?* Can you laugh at yourself and others? Do you enjoy working with others?
9. *Do you have a track record of success?* What contributions have you made in other areas of work or ministry?
10. *Can you handle evaluation and correction?* Can you take feedback in a mature manner? Or do you blow up when criticized? Are you willing to be subject to an annual review, which may include both positive and negative feedback?
11. *Are there embarrassments in your past?* Is there anything in your past that if made public would be an embarrassment to you and a liability to our team?
12. *Is your spouse in agreement with this decision?* Is your husband or wife enthusiastic about your filling this position? Does your mate

want to make this change, and will he or she support you in this new endeavor?

Don't surround yourself only with like-minded individuals; that creates a one-dimensional team. Variety is the strength of team leadership. Some of the people I have asked to join our team are my opposites in a number of areas. We disagree on many fine points and have widely varying personalities. I want them to be strong where I am weak. That is not a threat; it is an opportunity to build a stronger team. In spite of these differences mutual respect and common values hold us together. The glue that bonds us together is our deep-seated commitment to a common mission, an agreed-on vision, and mutual values. A leader who hires only people whom he perceives are weaker and less gifted than he is will stifle that organization.

Knowing what you want in building a team, the next question is, Where will you find them? At a recent forum sponsored by Leadership Network of Dallas, Texas, Lyle Schaller addressed the problem of finding competent leaders. "The critical issue in society is a shortage of competent leadership with the kind of passion that generates followers. This is also the critical issue for churches. What in your congregation are you doing to produce leaders for the next generation?"[6]

THE MASTER MENTOR

Producing leaders for the next generation should be on everyone's agenda. Just how we do that has much to do with mentoring. Mentoring is a relational experience. We cannot simply send people to class and expect them to come out mature leaders. Effective teams are not built with books, seminars, PC networks, or video series, but with sustained and prolonged human contact between leader and follower. This is the kind of contact the apostle Paul practiced. He wrote, "Finally, brothers, whatever is true, whatever is noble, whatever is right, whatever is pure, whatever is lovely, whatever is admirable—if anything is excellent or praiseworthy—think about such things. Whatever you have *learned* or *received* or *heard from me*, or *seen in me*—put it into practice. And the God of peace will be with you" (Phil. 4:8–9, italics added).

One of the problems in Christian leadership today is that a huge gap exists between what is communicated and what is lived out. Paul, however, consistently lived out what he preached to his followers. How do you know that I practice what I say in these pages? You don't, but the people working by my side know. This is the kind of personal impartation Paul was referring to. Not only had they heard him preach and teach; they also had watched his life as an open book. In fact, he urged them to put into practice the things they had seen in him.

When Paul imparted principles to his followers, he also lived them out. "So whether you eat or drink or whatever you do, do it all for the glory of God. Do not cause anyone to stumble, whether Jews, Greeks or the church of God—even as I try to please everybody in every way. For I am not seeking my own good but the good of many, so that they may be saved. Follow my example, as I follow the example of Christ. I praise you for remembering me in everything and for holding to the teachings, just as I passed them on to you" (1 Cor. 10:31–11:2).

Earlier in this same letter he wrote: "When I came to you, brothers, I did not come with eloquence or superior wisdom as I proclaimed to you the testimony about God. For I resolved to know nothing while I was with you except Jesus Christ and him crucified. I came to you in weakness and fear, and with much trembling. My message and my preaching were not with wise and persuasive words, *but with a demonstration of the Spirit's power,* so that your faith might not rest on men's wisdom, but on God's power" (2:1–5, italics added).

And to the Thessalonians Paul revealed his heart in these words: "We loved you so much that we were delighted to share with you not only the gospel of God but our lives as well, because you had become so dear to us. Surely you remember, brothers, our toil and hardship; we worked night and day in order not to be a burden to anyone while we preached the gospel of God to you. You are witnesses, and so is God, of how *holy, righteous and blameless we were among you who believed*" (1 Thess. 2:8–10, italics added).

Charles Swindoll explains that these passages show how the leader must not just preach principles; he must demonstrate them.

Did you catch what Paul said [in 1 Thess. 2:9–10] about his personal style? I don't want us to miss it, since it's a major secret of good leadership. He was pleased to impart "not only the gospel," but also "his life." With that kind of leader, you didn't have to settle for a truckload of truth dumped into your ears and nothing more. You also got, along with the truth, authentic reality—his own life. He had nothing to hide. Paul went on to say that he lived among his believers "uprightly and blamelessly." In other words "he practiced what he preached." Is it any wonder God was pleased to use this leader to such a remarkable extent? No pompous air about him. No distant, demanding despot who came, saw, and conquered. No visiting lecturer who remained aloof and lived in a world of touch-me-not secrecy. On the contrary, he was approachable, accessible, a leader who loved, whom people could get next to, whom God would use to shape the early history of his church.[7]

Paul was a master mentor. We learn from him that we cannot do leadership effectively while hiding behind our desks. This means we have to be vulnerable and to show others our lives. And the more people we are responsible to lead, the more others in a sense own us and restrict us. That is the price we have to pay for servant leadership that empowers others on the team to be successful.

A CODE OF TEAM CONDUCT

One night in Wheaton a powerful thunderstorm filled the night sky with heavenly fireworks. Lightning was everywhere. I actually enjoy these storms because my children get scared and cuddle and snuggle up to Donna and me for protection. The storm that night gave me a new insight into what conflict can do to bring a team's progress to a halt.

Living in the Midwest for a number of years has given me a unique appreciation for the steady flow of electricity. We in the Chicago area seem to be in the central path of thunderstorms and tornadoes each spring and fall. The snow and ice storms in the winter add to the odds that our electricity will be lost. Almost every winter we have to close our office a day or two because of power outages. On this particular night we went outside as the lights in our house began to flicker, to see if others in the neighborhood were losing electric power. Looking to the north we saw a most incredible light show taking place. The sky was lit up with bright yellow flashes, and we assumed a neighbor's house had caught fire.

As suddenly as the lights appeared, they vanished. Curiosity got the best of us, so we piled into the car and chased the light to its source with a spirit of great adventure. (What is it about fires and disasters that always attract us?) We saw that a large tree had been struck by lightning, and then banged into a light pole and knocked down wires, leaving several live wires dangling. The live wires had bounced around like an angered octopus, shooting huge arcs of electricity into the ground all around. It was as if the wires and ground were fighting each other for dominion.

This great light show had its downside. The conflict between tree, light-pole wires, and the ground knocked out electricity in hundreds of homes in the area for the night. A lot of expensive energy was lost that night, and many utility trucks were called in to tackle the problem.

Team conflict does the same thing—sparks fly as people clash. The next thing you know, everyone sees what is going on and then boom—the power is out. Instead of working together toward the common cause, the team is derailed into working out its internal problems.

Not long ago we had a major conflict between members in one of our teams overseas. At first it affected only two people, missionary wives. Soon we at the home office became aware of the strife and had to peel off some of our energy to deal with the situation. Then we learned that everyone on the team was being affected negatively by the tensions between the two. Then three became involved, then five, and soon the entire team on the field had taken sides. This situation grew like a snowball gathering size and momentum. As one thing led to another, the work slowed to a crawl while great amounts of time and energy were drained off to this side issue. Before it was over, we had to send in an outside team for conflict resolution. This kind of energy-draining conflict is one of Satan's greatest tools to slow down our impact.

At times we are called to be referees between players who have disagreements. I have certainly had times when people who work on my team have had lateral conflicts with other teammates. Who has not been in a staff meeting where heated words are exchanged? Differences of opinion should be openly allowed, but at times they can grow into unhealthy divisions between team members.

An essential part of mentoring a group is to preserve the team's unity.

Satan would love nothing more than to destroy our forward movement as a team by the roadblock of interpersonal strife. Conversely there is joy, peace, and productivity for the team that lives in harmony. As David wrote, "How good and pleasant it is when brothers live together in unity!" (Ps. 133:1). When workers are united, the engines of organization are firing on all eight cylinders and the work can move ahead.

The New Testament is filled with admonitions to have people living in unity, thereby showing the world that we are indeed different.

"I in them and you in me. May they be brought to complete unity to let the world know that you sent me and have loved them even as you have loved me." (John 17:23)

"May the God who gives endurance and encouragement give you a spirit of unity among yourselves as you follow Christ Jesus." (Rom. 15:5)

"Make every effort to keep the unity of the Spirit through the bond of peace." (Eph. 4:3)

"Until we all reach unity in the faith and in the knowledge of the Son of God and become mature, attaining to the whole measure of the fullness of Christ." (Eph. 4:13)

"And over all these virtues put on love, which binds them all together in perfect unity." (Col. 3:14)

Toward this end of maintaining unity on my leadership team, I have been working recently on a "Code of Conduct" for my senior staff. It expresses a set of values and principles to guide our behavior with each other. We have enjoyed tossing the concepts around, and just the topic itself has made for lively discussions. My suggestion is that you build such a code, with input from your team, and make it a moral contract between all of you. It says in effect, "We are committed to being an effective leadership team in the climate of mutual respect and mentorship." The following is our first attempt at the code.

A Leadership Team Code of Conduct

1. My personal success is measured by the success of our team.
2. We will practice *HOT* communications: *H*onest, *O*pen, and *T*ransparent.
3. I recognize that each member of our team has a special gift that contributes to the success of the whole group.
4. I will always speak positively of my teammates in public; they are safe with me even in their absence.
5. If I have a problem with a teammate, I will go to him or her first.
6. When in doubt, I will give my teammate the benefit of the doubt.
7. I will pray for each member of our team regularly.
8. We will support in public the decisions we have made in private.
9. Confidences will remain safely inside our group.
10. Grace will be given freely when we encounter one another's faults.

People everywhere are catching on to the need to express team values and leadership codes of conduct. Not long ago I had the opportunity to spend a day at a large ministry center in Orlando. A group of us were there for a day-long leadership workshop. I was delighted when I discovered the attractive banners and paintings that hung on the walls of the conference room where we met. Someone had taken a lot of time to frame ten words and phrases that admirably expressed the values of the people who regularly use that conference room. The ten were these: (1) listen, (2) confidentiality, (3) respect, (4) open communication, (5) believe the best, (6) safe environment, (7) unity, (8) speaking the truth in love, (9) God's Word, and (10) caring atmosphere.

Peter Drucker has had a profound influence on Bob Buford and the people at Leadership Network in Dallas, Texas. For the seventy-fifth issue of *NetFax*, their bimonthly newsfax, Buford chose what he and *Leadership Network* thought were ten of the most important lessons they have learned from Drucker. The list is a great example of the kind of thinking that challenges us to break out of our organizational paralysis and build dynamic leadership teams. Notice especially items seven, eight, and nine, which have to do with the team. Drucker agrees that leadership rises or falls on this issue of how we work together and lead our team.

Drucker's Top Ten Lessons

1. The mission comes first. The mission of nonprofits . . . . (including churches) is changed lives.
2. The function of management is to make the church more church-like, not to make the church more businesslike.
3. An organization begins to die the day it begins to be run for the benefit of the insiders and not for the benefit of the outsiders.
4. Know the value of planned abandonment; you must decide what not to do.
5. Know the value of foresight. You can't predict the future, but you must assess the futurity of present events.
6. Focus on opportunities, not problems. Most organizations assign their best resources to their problems, not their opportunities.
7. Management is a social function and has mostly to do with people, not techniques and procedures.
8. People decisions are the ultimate control mechanism of an organization. That's where people look to find out what values you really hold.
9. All work is work for a team. No individual has the temperament and the skills to do every job. The purpose of a team is to make strengths productive and weaknesses irrelevant.
10. The three most important questions are, What is our business? Who is our customer? What does the customer consider valuable? [8]

LEADERSHIP IS "WE"

In our individualistic world, we have to work at making teams function well. If leadership is best defined as leading a group that is working together, then the more I can let go of control and let the team lead, the better off we will be. Nothing destroys morale more than a "control freak"—the old-fashioned kind of leader who still wants to make all the decisions, call all the shots, and be the sole captain of the ship. Fortunately we have learned a great deal about leadership in the last few decades, so that this type of controlling leader is a dying breed. A control freak thinks he has all the answers, thinks he knows best because he was there first, has "founder-itis" (is unable to let go of what he started), delegates responsibilities but no authority to go with them, loves to control by keeping people in the dark, reverses decisions others have made, and doesn't give others room to make their own mark.

The great problem that caused the collapse of the Soviet Union was economic, not political; communism failed to believe in private ownership. Communist leaders were the world's worst control freaks. Everyone had a job but no one worked because there was no pride of ownership nor any incentive for personal productivity. Private ownership is an important key to human motivation, and because the central government controlled everything, people were not interested in building a productive society of responsible citizens.

To use another analogy, giving a co-leader a serious piece of the action with ownership authority is like moving from renting an apartment to owning your own home. Suddenly the pride of ownership kicks in, and personal motivation shoots skyward. When workers sense they have a degree of ownership in the organization, they realize they are not just punching a clock. They know they will be evaluated as individuals based on the quality of their work. They begin to see that their part in the organization can make a difference in the outcome of the group. When ownership stakes are raised, the followers' level of commitment soars proportionately. They can say with pride, "I did a great job!"

In creating a culture in which followers flourish, leaders must give members of the leadership team authority and ownership over some part of the work. A leader must quit looking over everyone's shoulders and give them freedom to work their plans on their own.

Isn't that what servant leadership is all about? Didn't Jesus model this pattern with His own style of leading? Jesus called the Twelve and trained them. Then He sent out the seventy-two and debriefed them when they returned. In the greatest act of delegation in history He departed after three years of training and left them to fulfill the Great Commission on their own. Talk about confidence!

I like what Herb Kelleherm, president of Southwest Airlines, says about letting go of control at his airlines.

> A financial analyst once asked me if I was afraid of losing control of our organization. *I told him I've never had any control and I never wanted it.* If you create an environment where the people truly participate, you don't need control. They know what needs to be done, and they do it. And the more that people will devote to your cause on a voluntary basis, a willing basis, the fewer hierarchies and control mechanisms you need. We're not looking for blind obedience. We're looking for people, who on their own initiative, want to be doing what they're doing because they consider it to be a worthy objective. I have always believed that the best leader is the best server. *And if you're a servant, by definition, you're not controlling.* [9]

In Jesus' three years of active ministry he found, selected, and trained twelve successors. When the time for the Crucifixion came, He had only a small bank of followers. But He set the pattern of what we call discipleship when He charged them to go fulfill what he had begun. "A new command I give you: Love one another. As I have loved you, so you must love one another" (John 13:34). "Again Jesus said, 'Peace be with you! As the Father has sent me, I am sending you' " (20:21). "Therefore go and make disciples of all nations, baptizing them in the name of the Father and of the Son and of the Holy Spirit, and teaching them to obey everything I have commanded you" (Matt. 28:19–20).

Discipleship is delegation. Jesus did not spread Christianity into a worldwide movement; His early followers did. The principle we see here is that He could not have accomplished His will without those who came after Him. In a similar way the members of our team—including those of the next generation—will most likely be the ones who will complete what we started.

DEVELOPING "GENERATION NEXT"

I mentioned in chapter 7 that the members of Generation X may stretch us to new places we may not want to go. Generation X, the population group that follows the Baby Boomers, is the approximately fifty million young Americans born between 1964 and 1977. Knowing the traits of this generation is essential if we are to lead them effectively and bring them along as the future leaders of our ministries. Sometimes as I look at the up-and-comers at CBI, I think, "Will he or she be on the leadership team that replaces me?" I don't take that as a threat but as a personal admonition to myself to be busy about the task of mentoring the new generation who will eventually take my place. Someday soon the young people of Generation X will be the leadership team of your organization. They will be taking over your church! That thought should not frighten you; instead it should motivate you to pave the way for them.

Generation X has been called the "Paradox Generation," because they display characteristics some of which stand in conflict with each other. Jeff Bantz, himself a "Gen X-er," lists these characteristics:

- Very individualistic, and yet, highly value relationships.
- Don't respect authority, yet long to receive instruction.
- Skeptical, yet pragmatic.
- Have an extended adolescence, and yet they grew up too soon.
- Slow to commit, and passionately dedicated.
- A challenge to manage, but are excellent workers.
- Apathetic, and yet care deeply.
- Relativistic and searching for meaning.
- Disillusioned, yet they are not giving up.
- A hazy sense of their own identity.
- Cynical, hopeless.[10]

Another group that studied Generation X made these observations about them:

- Disillusioned, skeptical of people in institutions.
- Feel they bear the consequences of the previous generation's greed and/or shortsightedness.
- Desire personal freedom and autonomy.
- Materialism is outwardly rejected but inwardly desired.
- Slow to assume responsibility for themselves or others.
- Feel they are the "have not" generation.
- Personal interests are more important than work or money.[11]

What do these characteristics mean for us who will assimilate these youth into leadership? A man who is blazing a trail of mentoring and helping develop the next generation of leaders is Leighton Ford. A decade ago he founded Leighton Ford Ministries for the purpose of identifying and developing emerging young leaders. Then in 1992 he began the Arrow Leadership program, which uses an innovative approach to train and mentor small groups of young leaders in evangelism leadership skills.

Ford writes this about today's present generation of forty- and fifty-year-olds who have replaced the World War II generation of leadership: "That generation of post-World War II leaders, which emerged on the national and international scene with tremendous vision and energy, has now largely moved off the stage. Interestingly, I do not see many visionary leaders in the late forties and fifties taking their places; those in that age range tend to be managers of their elders' visions in the organizations they had built. But I do see God raising up a new band of leaders among men and women who are under forty. . . ."[12]

When I first read these comments, I have to confess that they hurt because he was speaking to me about myself and my baby-boomer comrades. And yet I have to admit that there is truth to his words about my own generation of leadership. It is true that many managers are carrying on the traditions of our forefathers, but are not as visionary as we would like to see. Where are the future Bill Brights, Jill Briscoes, Billy Grahams, and Luis Palaus? Certainly the rigors of World War II helped inspire and create the fantastic arsenal of leaders that emerged on the world scene at the conclusion of that war. And conversely, the ease and softness of life in the developmental years of the boomers have made it more difficult for us to have the kind of character qualities Leighton Ford speaks of.

In an open letter to future leaders Ford gives nine points of advice for the under-forty crowd. These points are excellent advice for anyone involved in mentoring a team of future leaders.

Advice For Those Under Forty

1. Be "hopers." (Expect great things from God.)

2. Be "world Christians." (Stay keenly aware of what is happening all around the world, not just in North America.)

3. Be "visionaries like Jesus." (Vision is to see as God does, by reflecting prayerfully and biblically on what you see.)

4. Be "kingdom-seekers and not empire-builders." (Spend time building people, not your own ego.)

5. "Model the inclusiveness of Christ." (Respect people of the other gender and of an ethnicity that is not your own.)

6. "Have a pioneering spirit for the gospel." (Dream big dreams for God and seek to push out the gospel to new frontiers.)

7. "Stay attuned to the Holy Spirit." (Seek the presence of God's Spirit in an increasingly secular world.)

8. "Seek a heart for God." (May your doing for Christ always grow out of your being Christlike.)

9. "Hug an older leader." (As older leaders pass off the scene, love, respect, encourage, and spend time with your senior leaders.)[13]

The apostle Paul understood what flexibility and change is all about. He knew that mentoring a team of God's servants was the key to his success. He wrote, "So whether you eat or drink or whatever you do, do it all for the glory of God. Do not cause anyone to stumble, whether Jews, Greeks, or the church of God—even as I try to please everybody in every way. For I am not seeking my own good but the good of many [notice his good leadership team attitude], so that they may be saved. *Follow my example, as I follow the example of Christ*" (1 Cor. 10:31–11:1, italics added).

Recently I wrote a letter to a young Generation X couple who have become very dear to my wife and me. As we watch them develop into adulthood, we see in them many gifts as well as struggles. They are heading for a lifetime of ministry, and when they asked me about their future I shared with them these thoughts. I conclude this chapter with my letter to them.

Dear Glen & Cindy:

Thanks for asking for my advice on some of the things I think you should know about as you look forward to a life of ministry. Life is certainly full of changes for you this year. You've just completed your seminary training and had your first child after being married just a little over a year. Your whole life lies before you as a blank check which has not yet been written. Two decades ago, after Donna and I were married and completed seminary, we embarked on the road of ministry. Someone told me not long ago that only one out of every ten people who go into ministry actually retire from the pastorate. The dropout rate is discouraging.

I am happy to say that at the midpoint place where I find myself, which some people refer to as "half-time," I can look back on two decades of ministry and thank God for His faithfulness. And, as I look forward to twenty more years before I retire—if Jesus doesn't return or call me home before then—then I have every intention, by God's grace, to finish well.

"What have I learned about Christian leadership that I wish I had learned earlier?" I'm glad you asked. Actually, the short answer is that there are many things you simply have to learn through experience, things they can't teach you in seminary. Knowledge is one thing, but experience is something else. You can't front-load all the knowledge before you go through the experience of ministry. You simply have to take the knowledge you have and learn along the way. Even though there is no substitute for experience, let me give you some of the lessons I've learned along the way that I wish someone had told me earlier. I'll just bullet them for you and give you some comments under each topic. (These items are not in any order of priority.)

Nurture your life partner.

Never short-change the spouse God has given you for your ministry journey. I have made it a practice of always giving priority to my relationship with Donna. Through the years we've made it a habit of getting away on the average of once a quarter for at least one overnight stay in a hotel away from our children. These nurturing times have made a huge difference in our marriage. Once children come along, it is so easy for them to become the focus of the marriage. Then one day you find you've lost the spark that originally brought you together. Keep the spark alive, and don't fall into the trap of putting God's work before your responsibility to your spouse and family. Everything I have said about your spouse applies as well to your children. As God gives you children, be sure you don't sacrifice them for the sake of ministry. What does it profit a man if he gains the whole world and loses his children because of neglect?

Make people mentor you.

One of my greatest disappointments as I look back over my years of Christian ministry is the lack of mentorship in my life. A few men along the way have had a significant impact in my life, but even with them, I was disappointed that there wasn't as significant a relationship as I wanted. Very few people whom you may want to mentor you will actually take the initiative. It seems that those people you admire the most are the busiest and therefore don't have much time to mentor. If I had to do it over again, I would have been much more aggressive at seeking time with the people by whom I wanted to be mentored. I highly recommend that you develop mentoring relationships with people you want to be like.

Some people will let you down.

If I had to predict who would let me down, I would have missed every time. Just the people you think are always going to be there are the ones who may fail you. And then at times you are surprised by people you never expected to stand with you. I have learned through the years not to put my faith and trust for my future in people. This is not to say that we should be stubborn individualists, but that we should keep our eyes on Jesus, the Author and Finisher of our faith. Two close friends of mine both bailed out of their marriages through illicit affairs, tossing aside their spouses and children, and following the wiles of the flesh. That hurt very deeply. Of course, other Christian leaders have fallen, some of whom I used to look up to with great admiration. Some people you look up to from a distance will let you down, but also people who work close to you may at times be a disappointment. Expect it, and try to treat everyone with grace and forgiveness. When others let you down, you can always rely on your spouse, your family, and hopefully your closest friends. And remember that Jesus will not let you down.

Wait for leadership to come to you.

Don't set out with the intention of being a leader. Instead, be willing to serve Christ's church in any way you can. Leadership is something you may fall into after you've proven yourself as a follower. Don't get into the trap of not being willing to do the dirty work because you feel God has called you to be a leader. I find that leadership has a tremendous amount of dirty work and details that many followers don't want to mess with. You have to earn the right to lead by proving that you are a gracious and cooperative follower.

Accountability is not an option.

There are two sides to accountability. Personal accountability involves having a small cadre of friends with whom you can be transparent about every detail of your life. This is another area where I have failed in my life and would encourage you in. Having a small group of friends to whom you are accountable will go a long way toward helping protect you from the world, the flesh, and the devil. The second area of accountability is to the authority God has placed over you. I think it is imperative that people are accountable to someone. As the director of my organization, I am accountable to the board of directors. Some people in ministry have a spirit of independence, refusing to be accountable to anyone. This is not a healthy thing; it can create dangerous imbalance and irresponsibility. Submit yourself to those whom God has placed in authority over you.

Nurture your soul.

The older you get, the busier you'll get and the more the battle rages to find time to nurture your soul. Always make time to spend in the Word and in fellowship with your Savior. I have always loved D. L. Moody's statement: "Sin will keep you from the Bible, or the Bible will keep you from sin." Make time on a daily basis to cultivate and feed your soul, because from it springs character and integrity.

Nurture your body.

I am sad to say that as men grow older, many of them neglect their physical condition. Don't fall into the trap of adding a couple of pounds to your waist for every year of your life beyond age twenty-five. It is a poor testimony to church members and others for leaders to be overweight and underconditioned. Take good care of your body and it will have a very positive effect on your soul and spirit. Be careful what you eat, remember moderation in all things, and in the spirit of the apostle Paul learn to buffet your body and make it your slave.

Put people first.

Peter Drucker said, "Management is a social function and has mostly to do with people, not techniques and procedures."[14] Leadership is about people, so the key to successful Christian leadership is learning to get along with people and caring about people. Many young men and women who try to make a mark in Christian ministry fail because of their lack of people skills. Often these people tend to be gifted and brilliant. In fact, those who are highly gifted often fail in people skills because they rely on their gifts and abilities for success. I had a lot of failure in my own life in this area until I learned that leadership involves getting along well with people.

Don't fall into the age-discrimination trap.

It is disappointing that many organizations and churches today are no longer willing to look at anyone above the age of fifty as their potential leader. Whatever happened to the biblical concept of age and wisdom? Don't fall into that trap yourself. You have to realize that some things will not come to you until you have gained a certain age in life. By the time you are thirty or forty you can't have learned everything a sixty-year-old leader knows. You simply have to learn through years of experience. I really believe that is what the biblical concept of wisdom is all about. So learn to respect your elders, those people who are over fifty who still have a lot to contribute and teach us.

Pursue lifelong learning.

Never stop learning. In fact the two most important words in a leader's vocabulary are *listen* and *learn*. Never stop listening to people and never stop learning. Successful leaders are lifelong learners who believe there is always something new to learn. This means you should continue to develop the habit of reading different kinds of books, journals, and periodicals. It also means you need to continue to educate yourself by continuing education both formally and informally. The world changes so dramatically that we will never survive if we are not lifelong learners.

Let me finish my letter, Glen and Cindy, by answering the question, "How do you succeed in leadership?" I measure success by finishing well. At the end of his career, as he sat in a prison dungeon in Rome, Paul said, "I have fought the good fight, I have finished the race, I have kept the faith. Now there is in store for me the crown of righteousness" (2 Tim. 4:7–8). It is not over until it's over.

Finishing well is what success is all about. And how do you finish well? By maintaining personal and ministry integrity. This includes a lifelong positive outlook on your work. It also means you have developed mature relationships with those with whom you have worked. It is also measured by the quality of your relationship to your spouse and what kind of parent you were to your children. Maintain integrity in all your relationships both professionally and personally. I wish for you a lifetime of effective ministry, and if God wills, the privilege of leadership in the work of His vineyard.

Your friend and fan in Christ,
Hans

9
CREATIVITY

Cultivating Creativity in Leadership

> "For this is what the LORD says—he who created the
> heavens, he is God; he who fashioned and made the earth,
> he founded it; he did not create it to be empty, but formed
> it to be inhabited—he says: 'I am the LORD, and there is
> no other.'" (Isa. 45:18)

RECENTLY I sat in the lovely spacious home of Jack and Cheryl (not
their real names) on top of a beautiful mountain in their thirty-five-acre
spread. In his late fifties Jack gives much of his resources to help church-
related ministries. He made his millions by starting a company that was
eventually bought out by a bigger company. Lots of stock options and all
the rewards of his hard work followed. Jack is an intelligent man. I appreciate his wisdom and learned some valuable lessons from him in our couple
of hours together sipping coffee and talking by the warmth of his cozy
fireplace.

As we spoke of giving to the Lord's work and some creative ways to do
that, he commented to me, "Hans, why is it that Christians are always
behind the curve on new developments that the business world under-
stands right away? It seems that the church is always about fifteen years
behind."

Jack is right. The business and commercial world has to stay flexible
and master creativity and the change process just to stay alive, whereas
nonprofit organizations don't. As long as we keep convincing a few
people to give to our ministry, we can stay in business. We all know the
twenty/eighty rule in our churches: 20 percent of the people give 80
percent of the money to keep our ministries going. What if those 20

percent are just blindly loyal to us and not really holding our feet to the fire of effectiveness?

Jesus Christ told a parable to emphasize the truth that the world is often better than the Christian community at doing what God has called the church to do. In the parable of the shrewd manager Jesus noted that the world's sons often make wiser leaders than the sons of the kingdom. "The master commended the dishonest manager because he had acted shrewdly. For the people of this world are more shrewd in dealing with their own kind than are the people of the light" (Luke 16:8). Jesus commended the steward's astuteness, not his morality. Wisdom, not corporate ethics, was commended.

Some ministries should have dissolved years ago, but they stay alive and flounder because a few wealthy people either keep giving to them or leave them enough money in their estate to keep things afloat. Donna and I worked in one church years ago that was just that way. A few major trusts had been left behind to endow the ministry, and though the church had become completely marginalized in the community, the small remaining band of members took great pride in caring for the large facilities with these endowed dollars. They thought they were doing something of great kingdom significance, but I doubt it.

We and the government have a lot in common in this regard: It takes a lot to ever put us out of business. It fact it rarely happens, even with some of the most blatant examples of incompetence.

How can we combat institutional paralysis? By staying creative.

The longer we have been in business, the greater the probability that we don't really understand what's going on in the minds of our customers, our congregation, or our community.

We naturally think that we become experts through the years, but all those years can result in a certain isolation and conformity to traditions. We think we have the answers to people's questions, but they may well be questions people long ago quit asking. A sort of arrogance of tenure blocks many organizational leaders from seeing truths that are obvious to outsiders.[1]

He who never walks except where he sees other men's tracks will make no discoveries. Creativity forces us to look at old problems with new eyes. It makes us question the status quo and constantly look for improvements and enhancements to our ministries. It is about improving the quality of our work. The Total Quality movement has brought to America the helpful concept of continuous improvement—*Kaizen*, as the Japanese call it. *Kaizen* is the ability to make small improvements every day in our processes and products. In Japan every worker is expected to find some way each day to get just one-tenth of 1 percent improvement in what he does or makes.[2]

Old age is not an issue of hard arteries; it is a disease of rigid categories. As Henry Ford said, "Anyone who stops learning is old, whether at twenty or eighty. Anyone who keeps learning stays young. The greatest thing in life is to keep your mind young."[3]

A WOMAN WHO TOOK RISKS

Can you spot a creative person in the crowd? Not necessarily. After all, what is the essence of creativity? It has to do, I think, with new solutions to old problems. It means thinking in new ways and finding new approaches to solving problems. It is not necessarily flamboyance, colorfulness, or special giftedness.

God is the most creative of all in our universe and He made us in His image. Since He lavished such creativity on His work, shouldn't we also show creative beauty in our work?

Thinking of creative people in the Bible, many would gravitate quickly to David because of his strong gifts in music and poetry. Some might also think of Joseph or Job. And there is Moses, who had to look constantly for new creative ways to motivate God's people as he led them through their desert pilgrimage.

We have already seen in chapter 4 that Esther was a woman of great courage and encouragement. Now let's focus on her creativity. Part of what made her creative was her feminine nature, which always adds a dimension to leadership teams. I have worked hard at CBInternational to make a place for women in leadership, for, among other things, half our workers in the mission are women. Certainly they deserve to have issues related to their needs reflected in leadership discussions and decisions. But beyond that representation, I have found that having women in the leadership mix adds a dimension that we men would otherwise miss— and part of that dimension is creativity.

Being creative means "having the power or quality to create" or "having the quality of something created rather than imitated."[4] That is at the heart of creativity: the ability to come up with fresh new approaches to difficult situations or to improve routine situations. Twenty years ago I attended Robert Schuller's Institute of Church Leadership at the Crystal Cathedral in Garden Grove, California. To this day I remember vividly something he taught about creativity and problem-solving.

He told of moving to California and wanting to start a nontraditional church, where non-Christians would want to go and listen to the gospel. He decided to make a list of ten possible places where they could meet. The tenth place on his list happened to be a drive-in theater. Options one through nine fell through, so he was left with option ten. The drive-in church became such a sensation that others began to imitate him. He said that he didn't believe any problem was insurmountable. Every time you face a great problem, he suggests you make a list of ten possible solutions, no matter how bizarre they might seem. Then work your way down that list until you've come up with something that will work. That's creativity.

Esther is an excellent example of one who employed that kind of great creativity. Because of Haman's trickery and jealousy, King Xerxes proclaimed an edict that would annihilate the Jewish race. The fate of an entire nation was in the hands of Queen Esther!

At first she was terrified at the prospect of going before the king to ask for the Jews' safety, because by law no one was to approach the king without invitation. Her predecessor, Queen Vashti, had been deposed and banished for life from the king's presence for disobeying him! Esther was clearly aware of her precarious position. So she wisely implored Mordecai, her uncle, to gather all the Jews to fast and pray for her. She knew she must depend on God to open the way. The most quoted verse of Esther reads, "I will go to the king, even though it is against the law. And if I perish, I perish" (Esth. 4:16).

After waiting three days, Esther put on her royal robes and approached the king's court. He warmly received her, extending his scepter to her. Her courage in approaching the king made it obvious to him that she must have a very important request. At this point Esther could have taken the traditional, straightforward approach and just told the king outright of Haman's treacherous plot to destroy her and her people. Or she could also have revealed Mordecai's loyal gallantry at saving the king's life. But she chose to improvise, take her time, and allow the situation to unfold naturally. She asked the king if he and Haman would come to a banquet she had prepared for them. Probably the moment of greatest creativity for Esther happened at that banquet. For some reason, Esther did not sense that that banquet was the right occasion for revealing Haman's plot. So she asked if the king would come again the next day to another banquet she would prepare for him and Haman.

Impatience can be an enemy of creativity. That is, it takes time to be creative. The first solution that comes to mind is not necessarily the best one. We often go along with the first idea we hatch because we are busy and want to move on. But if we want the best solution, we need to ask others for input. This immediately slows down the process, which at times is difficult to do.

> *Lesson one of creativity in ministry: Take time to think of more than one solution to your problem. Rarely is the first instinct the best.*

Esther must have sensed that Haman was a dangerous enemy. She waited an extra day to make her request, and God worked out the situation during the night. Restless and unable to sleep, the king looked up some historical records and discovered that Mordecai was a great but unrewarded hero. Xerxes decided to honor him and ironically, the king ordered Haman, whose quiet rage continued toward Mordecai, to bestow the king's honors on Mordecai!

What rich irony is in this story. It reveals how God can turn evil intended against us for the greatest good. Esther's dependence on God is evident, and her creativity in presenting her case to the king paid off, probably far beyond her expectations! In a sense Haman hanged himself by preparing gallows for Mordecai, conveniently completed just in time, on the day of the second banquet. Also during the second banquet the king urged Esther to tell him her request. So she asked the king to prevent the slaughter of herself and her people, the Jews. The king immediately responded with rage and demanded to know who had devised the scheme!

So Esther's petition was granted. Haman was hanged on the gallows he had built for Mordecai, and the Jews were given authority by the king to destroy all their enemies. God used this creative woman to preserve His people. Her creativity focused on being sensitive to God's leading in her life. What lessons of creativity can we learn from her?

CHRISTIAN ENTREPRENEURS?

Someone has said that revolutions throw people into three different roles or modes of performance: those who lead the revolution, those who follow it, and those who sleep through it. "These days," says Karl Albrecht, "the sleepers are in real trouble. What you don't know can kill you."[5] We cannot be asleep at the wheel of our organizations in times like these.

Creativity should be the name of the game for us in Christian leadership positions. Creative leadership does involve significant risk-taking. After all, in the words of hockey great Wayne Gretzky, "You miss one hundred percent of the shots you don't take." Whether we are leading a church, a parachurch ministry, a Christian business, or are involved in Christian music or publishing, our work should be marked by a refreshing God-driven creativity. God, the greatest of all the creative ones in His universe, never runs out of creativity—nor should we. Those who take risks for His purposes find that He is faithful in making big things happen.

Each year the consulting firm of Ernst and Young sponsors the Entrepreneur of the Year Award. This award recognizes ingenuity, hard work, and the special skills that it takes to create, build, and sustain a successful business in today's competitive climate. Wouldn't it be great to see a Christian Ministry Entrepreneur of the Year Award granted to those who are working hard in the trenches to carve out ministries that make a difference in today's world?

Creativity is certainly not a domain dominated by the young. In fact recent winners of the Ernst and Young Award went to father-and-son team Jack Taylor, age seventy-five, and Andy Taylor, age fifty, founders of Enterprise Rent-a-Car. The company was honored because of its creative culture, in which each employee is treated as an individual entrepreneur. This type of culture has allowed Enterprise to become one of the top car-rental companies in America, with one new location opening every day!

In the business world today's heroes are no longer the chief executive officers who climb to the top of the established corporate ladder, but those people such as Herb Kelleherm, of Southwest Airlines, who built it all from scratch, or Bill Gates, who became unimaginably rich in unimaginably little time. Today's entrepreneurs are receiving more affirmation than ever before. Not long ago people who started their own businesses, planted new churches, or began new ministries were not accorded the same public respect as doctors, lawyers, or heads of corporations. But in today's climate entrepreneurs are being looked on as trendsetters. They are the heroes, especially to members of Generation X.

More than ever before, conditions are ripe for creativity and cutting-edge freshness in Christian leadership.

With the frantic pace of change, anything less than new solutions will leave us with less than top-level efficiency. We will watch from the sidelines as those who have made the changes reap the rewards of their flexibility. Some of today's heroes are those like Bill Hybels, who created a megachurch ministry, reaching the unchurched masses in the western suburbs of Chicago, or Rick Warren, who accomplished a similar feat in the foothills of Orange County in southern California. They employ wonderful creativity without compromising the clear truth of the gospel. Entrepreneurship is "where it's at" and creativity is the key to entrepreneurship.

FINDING YOUR LEADERSHIP FIT

Not every creative leader is an entrepreneur. In fact it would be suicide for an organization to have only that kind of leader. Part of the task of leading a team is to help each member find and use his or her gifting and personality style. Not long ago I took my senior leaders on a retreat to work through the DISC test profile. Of the ten of us, three came out as "High D's" (Dominance pattern). A few are I's (Inspiration), S's (Steady) and C's (Control and Conformity). If we were all the same, we would have a weak leadership team. I want our treasurer, for example, to be a High C (which he is), because careful control is most important in his job. He does not need to be reckless with the finances! We also need "people persons" who like standing around the water cooler chatting with anybody and everybody.

There are many ways of looking at leadership styles. Based on his years of observing various leaders in the church, Bill Hybels has developed ten leadership styles. If a man or woman has the gift of leadership, it manifests itself, he says, in one of these ten ways. This analysis is helpful when building your team and examining where different leaders in your organization fit.

Leadership Styles

- *Visionary leader,* who has crystal-clear pictures of where the ministry should be heading
- *Directional leader,* who can carefully sort through complex issues of direction for the ministry at any given moment
- *Strategic leader,* who forms the game plan to help make the vision become a reality
- *Managing leader,* who organizes the nuts and bolts that move us along the road to our destination
- *Motivational leader,* who knows how to fire up the troops and keep morale high
- *Shepherding leader,* a nurturing person who makes sure people's needs are met
- *Team-building leader,* who places people in the right positions and helps coach the players on the team
- *Entrepreneurial leader,* a start-up person with energy, vision, and a risk-taking spirit

- *Re-engineering leader,* who can make an old organization new again
- *Bridge-building leader,* the politican type who builds multiple alliances to get the job of leadership done[6]

Hybels shares his concern about a certain amount of "gift envy" among church leaders today. If we recognize that the church will look different on every street corner and in every nation, and that we need all kinds of leaders to be effective, then we can avoid this unnecessary competitive envy.

It is important for ministry leaders to know where creative ideas will come from. If you have one or two creative leaders on your team, that will become their major contribution to the whole. If you are not creative, be sure you have some on your senior staff who are. And be sure you listen to them—as opposed to squashing their enthusiastic ideas! It is worth repeating here this favorite statement on creativity and change: "In times of change, learners inherit the earth, while the learned find themselves beautifully equipped to deal with a world that no longer exists."

POLICY VERSUS PASSION

Jerry Rankin, a great leader I have had an opportunity to come to know in recent years, is the president of the International Mission Board of the Southern Baptist Convention, the largest mission sending agency in the United States. Recently he introduced radical creative change into the worldwide ministry of that mission. This has caused shifts in organizational structure of earthquake proportions. Jerry took his time to study the organization for several years before introducing his massive program of change, and he felt the time was right for a creative new start. He stated:

> Our organization and leadership must be flexible, responsive, and innovative to flow with the continuous change and opportunities we will encounter in the future. We must empower each missionary to maximize his or her potential and to fulfill his or her calling rather than maintaining the traditions of an organization and in any way allowing our policies and procedures to restrict and inhibit effectiveness.
>
> We must propagate a shared vision that creates a passion to bring the

lost to Jesus Christ and reach all the peoples of the world. This vision cannot be pushed down from the top, but must be embraced by every individual. . . . We must nurture innovation and risk-taking, encourage mobility and absolutely eliminate any vestige of provincialism if we are to make a global impact.

We need to release our leaders to lead rather than being bogged down by a glut of administrative tasks, seeking to control and enforce conformity to policies and structures. We need to liberate leadership to cast the vision, inspire and mobilize the energies of missionaries working in concert with national partners and diminish the necessity of managing of the mission.[7]

Now those are the words of a creative risk-taker! What do you suppose is the reaction among the rank and file to the changes Rankin is imposing from the top down? To say the least, there is less than an enthusiastic response in every sector of the organization. His creativity sounds lofty on paper, but many people run for cover when they see statements like this–fearing for their jobs and their power.

Why is this? It's because as they grow older people tend to stray away from creativity and toward institutional conformity. They move from passion for their calling to protectionism for their existence. We have to guard carefully against falling into this trap.

Hallmarks of Creative Leaders

- passion, not policy
- inspiration, not institution
- apostolic fervor, not mechanistic function
- creativity, not control
- empowerment, not management
- focus on the future, not fear of failure

HOW TO PROMOTE CREATIVITY

Ideas are probably our most valuable resource. *Ideas are the currency of the future.* This intellectual capital—innovation, imagination, and creativity—must be valued and sought at all costs. Percy Barnevick, chairman of the giant ABB corporation, says that his first and foremost challenge as a leader is "releasing the brain power."[8] Bennis and Nanus say that to keep organizations thriving, "leaders must be instrumental in creating a social architecture capable of generating intellectual capital."[9]

In the summer of 1993 the Oregon Trail celebrated its one hundred and fiftieth anniversary. Partly motivated by the anniversary and fueled by our spirit of adventure, our family of six climbed into our motor home and set off to retrace the steps of those early American pioneers. The Oregon Trail stretches for two thousand miles, halfway across the United States from Independence, Missouri, to Oregon City, Oregon. At both ends of the trail and all along the route, there are informative interpretive centers. We soon learned of the many who died while trying to make this trip in covered wagons. "Oregon fever" broke out in the spring of 1843, and soon one thousand men, women, and children gathered at Independence with their wagons to make the six-month trek. Of the six thousand people who set out between 1843 and 1846, one thousand died along the way. Yet tales of hardship did not deter the early pioneers who settled the Pacific Northwest.

As we stood in some of the actual wagon ruts of those early Americans, we kept asking ourselves, "Why did they do it?" and "Would we have done it?" Why they went is clear to all who know the history of our country. They were looking for a better life, a fresh start, greener pastures, and freedom. Yes, we believed, the Finzel family would have certainly gone along on the journey.

There are always times in the lives of our churches when we need a fresh start. We need the kind of pioneering spirit that characterized those early settlers. To seek to improve their lives they risked much, and we must do the same. Peter Drucker says every organization needs to discover which risks it can afford to take, which risks it cannot afford to take, and *which risks it cannot afford not to take.*

Perhaps not everyone was cut out for the Oregon Trail. But creativity and risk in our organizations are not just for the gifted few. It is a necessary component of every learning organization. Your church needs creativity. Your ministry needs creativity. Are there any significant ways in which your ministry is doing its work differently from five years ago? Are you looking for new means of ministry? If not, you have a problem. Becoming a learning organization is essential today. Learning and the creative change process are one and the same.

"The real voyage of discovery consists *not* in seeking new landscapes but in having new eyes," says Marcel Proust.[10]

Promoting Creativity in Your Organization

- Reward creativity and pioneering
- Allow new blood into the leadership
- Provide cross-training and conferencing
- Have networking
- Visit those who do it right
- Allow failure; encourage trial and error
- Read outside your field
- Listen to the troops
- Bring creative people into leadership
- Make it safe to be creative in your organization
- Celebrate creative acts in your group
- Relax the controls that stifle coloring outside the lines.

How safe is it to be creative in your group? Is change rewarded or is preserving the rituals of tradition the preferred behavior? Do your people know what you value? Can you articulate your culture for everyone to see it? As you initiate new people into your ranks, can you let them know clearly what you stand for? Would every one of the leaders in your organization tell the same story? Ralph Kilmann writes this about the power of corporate culture: "The organization itself has an invisible quality—a certain style, a character, a way of doing things—that may be more powerful than the dictates of any one person or any formally documented system. To understand the essence or soul of the organization requires that we travel below the charts, rulebooks, machines, and buildings into the underground world of corporate cultures."[11]

Creativity must be a part of your formal organizational culture for it to be encouraged and unimpeded. At CBInternational we have fostered a pioneering spirit by putting our values out in the open for everyone to see. It is very much a part of our corporate culture. We have tried to make it a part of our formal written statements of mission and values. Our appreciation of creativity can be seen in our mission statement, which is printed in our literature and is framed in the entry area of our offices. In our mission statement we encourage free thinking and pioneering.

CBInternational Mission Statement

"In vital partnership with churches at home and abroad, the mission of CBInternational is to be a pioneering force in fulfilling Christ's Commission to the final frontiers of the harvest."

In addition to our mission statement we have developed a set of four core values that guide us along the way. These core values were shaped a number of years ago and have helped guide us in making strategic decisions about how we relate to each other in our organization.

The Core Values of CBInternational

Values create, shape, and perpetuate the ethos of an organization. In pursuit of CBI's objectives, the following underlying values characterize every aspect of CBI's endeavor as it relates to the members of our organization:

1. Individual Dignity

We diligently maintain and promote the dignity and worth of each individual within CBI's ministries worldwide. People with a proper sense of spiritual and emotional well-being are freed for productive ministry that is committed to goal-oriented planning and team accountability.

2. Corporate Creativity

We encourage creative and innovative strategies directed by the Spirit of

God and implemented through policies and structures that are characterized by mutual trust and cooperation.

3. Uncompromising Integrity

We adhere uncompromisingly to honesty and integrity in all matters pertaining to the missions enterprise, whatever the consequences. This will always be manifested by biblical standards of ethics, morality, and financial accountability wherever CBInternational's personnel are involved.

4. Personal Development

We are committed at all levels of leadership to create an organizational climate conducive to continuing personal growth and development in missionary service. Management is implemented as a ministry of enablement and encouragement.

The workers or members of your organization will immediately sense how much the leadership respects them. Treat them like cogs in a machine, mere "worker ants," and their loyalty and productivity will be low. But give them respect and the dignity they deserve, and they will be ready to do anything for you. Of course, *respect must be genuine; it cannot be faked.* By allowing your people creative room to dream and perhaps sometimes fail, you are saying that their input is critical to the success of your ministry.

Our nine strategic priorities at CBI help guide our daily decisions about the things to which we will commit ourselves as an organization. Some churches and other Christian ministries get into trouble not for attempting too little but for attempting too much. Concentration is the key to success, and sometimes just the busyness of too many commitments dilutes our sharp effectiveness. Priorities can help confine us to what is critical. Notice that priorities eight and nine have to do with creativity and pioneering.

CBI's Nine Strategic Priorities

1. Evangelizing the unreached peoples of the world
2. Discipling a new generation of national leadership
3. Mobilizing national Christians for effective ministry
4. Planting vibrant local churches
5. Offering help to the poor and suffering

6. Entering restricted-access nations
7. Evangelizing the great urban centers of the world
8. Anticipating the open doors of tomorrow
9. Applying innovation to the mission strategies of tomorrow

At CBI we have developed another set of guidelines, a set called "How to Score at CBI." Every church and organization has its unique way of doing things. After I spent two years in the executive role at CBI, one of my key leaders asked me to put down in writing what I value most from our followers. I appreciated her request and the following is the result, now handed out broadly throughout our organization:

How to Score at CBI

Demonstrate belief in CBI's mission, vision, and values
  • Believe in CBI's mission and vision—memorize our mission statement
  • Have a passion for growth—it's a sign of abundant life
  • Think of new ways for CBI to fulfill its mission and to do it more effectively

Be a CBI pioneer
  • Take risks to accomplish greater things
  • Develop a pioneer mentality for problem-solving
  • Display creativity and innovation in your work area—new ways to approach old problems
  • Generate new ideas that work to make things better
  • Strive daily for continuous improvement
  • Push the technology envelope; work smarter

Practice excellence
  • Care about a high standard of excellence
  • Set standards; don't just follow what others do
  • Develop a disdain for mediocrity
  • Promote the use of state-of-the-art graphics and publications
  • Strive for "customer" satisfaction: our donors, pastors, missionaries, and nationals

Keep It Simple
- Reduce paperwork and increase efficiency
- Simplify bureaucracy and fight institutionalism
- Flat organizations work better; reduce layers of decision-makers
- Practice the *ODD* approach: Outsource, Downsize, and Deconstruct layers of inefficiency
- Ask for authority to make more decisions that affect you

Promote a team mentality; "we" is better than "me"
- Develop ways to work in teams
- If you lead, delegate!
- Whether you lead or follow, communicate!
- If you lead, empower others
- If you lead, push responsible decision-making downstream
- Recognize that teams come up with the greatest ideas
- Display a kingdom mentality
- Don't be concerned with who gets the credit
- Share the blessing with others; don't worry about "turf"
- Have a kingdom mentality; don't beat the denominational drum
- Give outsiders what they request
- Network, network, and network
- Help create a fun place to work
- Believe that work is fun
- Avoid whining at all costs
- Show grace with everyone inside and out
- Be positive and encourage a job well done

These value statements put right out in the open what our leaders value from our people. It legitimizes creativity. It helps create a set of values that provide a fresh pioneering atmosphere for us all to enjoy. Hopefully by being this kind of pioneer we will be more effective in fulfilling our mission.

Creativity in ministry is needed today more than ever, and not just because of the changing times in which we live.[12] We need to allow younger generations coming into our churches and organizations to color outside the lines we have drawn—to have their own chance to put their mark on the ministries God has given us. One day they will be responsible to take up the mantle and lead, and they will certainly not do it the way we did. Let them take risks now while yet under your leadership, for the day will come when they will no longer have us by their side to help them learn from their mistakes.

The Dilemma
by Ann Landers

To laugh is to risk appearing a fool.

To weep is to risk appearing sentimental.

To reach out to another is to risk involvement.

To expose feelings is to risk rejection.

To place your dreams before the crowd is to risk ridicule.

To love is to risk not being loved in return.

To go forward in the face of overwhelming odds is to risk failure.

But risks must be taken because the greatest hazard in life

is to risk nothing. The person who risks nothing does nothing,

has nothing, is nothing.

He may avoid suffering and sorrow, but he cannot learn, feel,

change, grow or love. Chained by his certitudes, he is a slave.

Only a person who takes risks is free.[13]

10
LIFE CYCLES OF LEADERS
Seasons in a Life of Leadership

"I have fought the good fight, I have finished the race, I have kept the faith." (2 Tim. 4:7)

O N   A   R E C E N T   V I S I T to the beautiful city of Rome, I received a fresh and deep impression about the apostle Paul. Seeing what conditions he faced at the end of his life made me appreciate all that much more that he finished well. Every leader I talk with readily admits that they earnestly want to finish well. We want it and Paul showed how it is done.

Though Paul's leadership was well known throughout the ancient church in and around Rome, I am not sure how many people who visit Rome today have any idea who he was, although he was one of the church's greatest leaders. Traces of him are scarce in modern-day Rome.

Any visitor to Rome learns immediately that St. Peter's Church is at the center of the city's attractions. Like magnets, the Vatican, St. Peter's Basilica, and the beautiful museums that surround it draw millions to this ancient city each year. I visited Vatican Square, toured St. Peter's Cathedral, and spent half a day in the Vatican Museum. I was especially impressed by the works of Michelangelo in the Sistine Chapel. However, what inspired me most about my visit to Rome happened after I left those great buildings and that rich history. As impressive as they are, there was something more special in store.

On an obscure side street a few kilometers from the Vatican, there is a small building thought to house the prison cell where Paul spent his final days. Whether it is actually his prison cell or not is of course debatable. We climbed down into this cramped hole beneath the ground and spent about a half-hour in the dark cell. It was cold, damp, and musty. A small grate in the ceiling allowed a little daylight to shine through. Historians agree that Paul probably lost his life around A.D. 67 when Nero ruled.

As I sat on that cold stone floor, I imagined what it must have been like for Paul in those last days. If this wasn't the exact room, it had to be just like it. What a way to spend your final weeks. As we stood in the cell and talked, drinking in the story that the stones could tell if they spoke, we noticed that only a few visitors climbed down into the cell with us. This was in stark contrast to the thousands who waited in line to enter the Vatican Museum not far away. The streets above were filled with tourists who were flocking to St. Peter's Cathedral, but only occasionally did someone stop long enough to even peer through the grate down into the cell. I thought to myself, "Here is where the man who wrote the greatest portion of the New Testament spent his last days. The greatest missionary and church planter of the first century died here. Wouldn't more people want to feel what it was like for him?" Obviously the answer is no. Most people visiting Rome today do not list Paul's cell as one of their top ten tourist sites. But for me it ranked as the number-one spot in Rome.

The words Paul wrote in his prison cell in those last days filled my heart as I contemplated his lifetime contribution to the church. He had sacrificed a great deal, but the reward was worth it. This passage came to my mind: "For I am already being poured out like a drink offering, and the time has come for my departure. I have fought the good fight, I have finished the race, I have kept the faith. Now there is in store for me the crown of righteousness, which the Lord, the righteous Judge, will award to me on that day—and not only to me, but also to all who have longed for his appearing" (2 Tim. 4:6–8).

Here is where he finished well. I silently prayed to the Lord, "That's what I want to do somewhere, someday Lord—to finish well as Paul did, but hopefully, however, not in a cell like this." Paul had made it to the end of his life and he knew it. He had a bumpy start, he learned much about maturity in his middle years, he accomplished incredible tasks during the height of his missionary ministry, and he was now showing what it meant to finish well. Could he have written what he wrote without the painful experiences he went through? I doubt it. We have the glib saying in our modern culture, "No pain, no gain." But Paul wrote the original bestseller on gain through pain centuries ago. As he was defending his apostleship to the Corinthian church, against his own personal desire, he took the time to summarize some of the costs he had to pay as a great leader.

> Are they servants of Christ? . . . I am more. I have worked much harder, been in prison more frequently, been flogged more severely, and been exposed to death again and again. Five times I received from the Jews the forty lashes minus one. Three times I was beaten with rods, once I was stoned, three times I was shipwrecked, and I spent a night and a day in the open sea. I have been constantly on the move. I have been in danger from rivers, in danger from bandits, in danger from my own countrymen, in danger from Gentiles; in dangers in the city, in danger in the country, in danger at sea; and in danger from false brothers. I have labored and toiled and have often gone without sleep; I have known hunger and thirst and have often gone without food; I have been cold and naked. Besides everything else, I face daily the pressure of my concern for all the churches. Who is weak, and I do not feel weak? Who is led into sin, and I do not inwardly burn? If I must boast, I will boast of the things that show my weakness. (2 Cor. 11:23–30)

Paul was a survivor; He finished well. He used his tough experiences to defend his apostleship. Paul's trials were an integral part of how God used Paul; they helped to validate his leadership over the long haul. Those trials were part of the cost of being all he needed to be as God's man in the hour in which God called him to lead. Perhaps it was because Paul had such experiences of suffering that he was able to end his game so victoriously.

> *Who ever said finishing well gets easier the closer you get to the end?*

How much did the hardships in Paul's life condition him for the end game? The great price he paid for his leadership role was to end his life in that dark, damp, lonely prison cell.

163

J. Oswald Sanders wrote of the price of leadership: "No one need aspire to leadership and the work of God who is not prepared to pay a price greater than his contemporaries and colleagues are willing to pay. True leadership always exacts a heavy toll on the whole man, and the more effective the leadership is, the higher the price to be paid."[1]

Paul paid that price and concluded his life with a sterling testimony. From his early days as a zealous missionary to the final days of his apostolic leadership, the seasons of his life serve as examples to us.

A final lesson we need to observe in the pursuit of effective leadership is to recognize that leadership has its seasons. Since our goal is to finish well, then we must traverse each stage of life intact. Unfortunately this doesn't always happen. Steve Farrar has observed that it is the *rare* man who finishes strong, it is the *exceptional* man who finishes strong, and it is the *teachable* man who finishes strong.[2]

Yet many around us have made it to the finish line successfully. This chapter examines the seasons of leadership and key issues we need to master in order to reach that goal line of finishing well. Paul gives us lessons of hope along the way—he made it under the worst of circumstances.

Just as each year has its seasons, so the life of every leader goes through seasons of leadership. We begin with the early start-up years of youthful enthusiasm and faith, followed by the stretching middle years that can make or break us, and then the rewards of heightened effectiveness in the maturing years of ministry. We'll take a look at all three of these times of the life of a leader and some of the signposts along the way that can help us navigate them successfully. No matter when God decides it is time for us to finish our journey on earth, we should be wanting to end well. This chapter concludes with a discussion of the barriers and hallmarks of finishing well.

THE START-UP YEARS

Nothing is quite so refreshing to an older leader as to see the youthful zeal and spark of a young leader launching out with idealism and energy. Our early experience in ministry can be like the launching of a rocket. The trouble is, not all those rockets stay in orbit. And some young leaders don't last beyond their start-up years.

I have loved rockets and space exploration all my life, having been infected at an early age by my father who spent his career building missiles. During the final desperate years of World War II, my dad and his boss, Wernher von Braun, and several thousand German scientists and engineers were busy at a secret rocket installation in northern Germany, developing, testing, and building the first intercontinental missile, known as the V-2.

As the war was winding down, von Braun made a decision to flee to the Western front, purposely, to be captured by the Americans. In the summer of 1945 the United States captured him and a hundred other men, including my dad, and brought them to America. With them they shipped dozens of the V-2's, which were later fired in the White Sands desert in New Mexico. The U.S. Government wanted to learn all they could about building rockets from this band of immigrants. Within two years the wives and children joined their husbands and fathers in Texas and the United States space program was about to be born.

The problem with those early rockets was that many started with an impressive launch only to end up nose down in the sand. They were duds. After my parents moved to Huntsville, Alabama, where I grew up and where NASA got its start, there were many disappointing days in the early years of the race to the moon when the rockets would fail. The funny thing about a dud is that you never really knew it was one as it sat on the launching pad. It looked good, but so many things could go wrong. A certain number of every batch of rockets they built in those years were duds.

I don't want to end up like one of dad's dud rockets, with my nose down in the sand, expended, useless, and a huge disappointment to those who were counting on me. My burning passion is to have success at the other end of the flight, fulfilling God's objectives for me and accomplishing all that He intended me to do while on this earth. That thought brings me right back to Paul and his words in prison: "Not that I have already obtained all this, or have already been made perfect, but I press on to take hold of that for which Christ Jesus took hold of me. Brothers, I do not consider myself yet to have taken hold of it. But one thing I do: Forgetting what is behind and straining toward what is ahead, I press on toward the goal to win the prize for which God has called me heavenward in Christ Jesus" (Phil. 3:12–14).

The best way to finish well is to *begin with the end in mind*. We all know of Paul's very dramatic beginning to his ministry. On the way to Damascus, where he planned to arrest every Christian he could find, he was stopped in his tracks, confronted with a vision of the Lord Jesus Christ. After walking blind for three days—it took a lot to get Paul's attention!—he received God's call for ministry through the words of Ananias: "But the Lord said to Ananias, 'Go! This man is my chosen instrument to carry my name before the Gentiles and their kings and before the people of Israel. I will show him how much he must suffer for my name'" (Acts 9:15–16).

Hearing God's call on his life, Paul did take off like a rocket in his zeal to be a diligent worker in this new harvest field. His early progress was truly remarkable for a young man fresh into the ministry. He is every mentor's dream come true. "Yet Saul *grew more and more powerful* and baffled the Jews living in Damascus by proving that Jesus is the Christ" (9:22, italics added).

But there needed to be a proving and growing time for Paul. This time of deepening began when believers sent him back home to Tarsus, to spend some time growing up in the faith outside the limelight of ministry (9:30; Gal. 1:1—2:1). This same experience of having a quiet period for growth and development is common among other great biblical leaders. It happened to Joseph, Moses, and David, to name a few. Jesus Himself had a proving and developing time as an adult, before beginning his lifework at thirty years of age. Similar growth is needed by many young zealous leaders.

Two years after Paul's conversion, he dropped out of sight for what became known as the silent years he spent in Tarsus. Peter became the focus of the Book of Acts until Paul resurfaced in Acts 13, years later. From A.D. 36 to about A.D. 46, Paul was maturing and growing in his faith privately in a part of the story that is not revealed to us. In fact he received a second call when the maturing and testing time was over, a call for ministry. "While they were worshiping the Lord and fasting, the Holy Spirit said, 'Set apart for me Barnabas and Saul for the work to which I have called them'" (13:2).

The first call of Paul in Acts 9 was to ministry in general, followed by a maturing time. But now in Acts 13 he was ready to be set apart for specific public ministry, and the pressure cooker began. What did God accomplish in Paul during those quiet years? Although we don't know for sure, I believe Paul was learning at least four things. First, he learned the power of *prayer,* how to draw strength from his new Lord and Commander. He needed to draw strength from his vertical relationship with God before he engaged in horizontal ministry to men and women.

Second, he learned *patience,* how to wait on God till He gives the signal to "go." Action-oriented Paul had to learn to let His new Chief be the Initiator of his ministry activities.

Third, he learned the *promises of God* in the Scriptures and how they related to his calling. He knew the Old Testament as well as any good Pharisee, but no doubt he studied it afresh with new eyes after his conversion and call to ministry.

Fourth, he learned the importance of a *proven character.* Certainly God was working in Paul's heart to break him of some of his bad pharisaic habits and to build in him the character he needed to lead the church through its great expansion period.

In November 1996 *Christianity Today* celebrated its fortieth anniversary by devoting an issue to "Up & Comers." Recognizing the passing of the baton from the World War II era of leaders to the next generation, *Christianity Today* editors wrote, "In this issue we look to those 40 and under who are now taking the reins of leadership. All are bright, talented visionaries and doers, and each seeks the Spirit's leading."[3]

It was a great issue, and I couldn't help but think statistically about these fifty promising young faces that filled their pages. Where will they be twenty years from now? I hope *Christianity Today* does a twenty-year follow-up, and I hope the report is a good one. It was an encouraging thing to see such promising talent and energy taking over leadership in evangelicalism. These men and women are truly starting with big impact!

THE MIDDLE YEARS

Leaders in their middle years—in their forties—are about twenty years out with twenty left to go. These years are much like the middle of a marathon. Remember the marathon I mentioned running while living in Vienna? I did actually complete the twenty-six miles to the finish line, thanks to Donna who would not let me give up. Without question, the middle was the hardest. Beginning was euphoric, and the end was pure adrenaline as I saw the finish line within view. But in the middle I got tired and discouraged and almost gave up hope that I would have what it would take to finish. I felt like quitting; I felt that completing the race was just not worth the sacrifice. And I looked at all those people on the sidelines; they were content to be spectators. Why wasn't that good enough for me?

In the middle years of Paul's ministry he was busy about his missionary journeys. He was a hardworking man. And like Paul, in our middle years we have to work the hardest as leaders. Usually the greatest weight of what we will ever bear will be on our shoulders by then. Several times Paul revealed the passion of his heart that was driving him forward to fulfill his vision. "We proclaim him, admonishing and teaching everyone with all wisdom, so that we may present everyone perfect in Christ. To this end I labor, *struggling with all his energy, which so powerfully works in me*" (Col. 1:28–29, italics added).

It is important to note that although Paul *was* a hardworking, driven man, he was constantly aware of his complete and utter dependence on the power of the Lord Jesus Christ. He did not attempt great things for God on his own. This cannot be emphasized strongly enough. If Paul had forged ahead in these middle years as a missionary, church planter, and writer on his own strength alone he would have burned out and given up. Instead he drew on the deep well of the energy and power of his Lord, fully aware that his work was God's work. We can step ahead in our middle years as leaders only if we know we are walking in complete dependence on the leading and strength of our Lord.

Was Paul successful in these middle ministry years? Of course. Forming a riot to get rid of Paul and his companions, unbelievers in Thessalonica said, "These who have turned the world upside down have come here too" (Acts 17:6 NKJV). What greater compliment could anyone have paid them?

Something seems to happen to people in their forties, something we label "the midlife crisis." Call it what you will, it's a time when we realize we are probably living our dreams at the present time. We know who we are and sense our weaknesses more than ever.

No matter what we may at one time have hoped and dreamed we would become, what we are now is most likely what we will be to the end.

During these days we must learn to be content with where God has planted us. The disillusionment and disparity between the early dream and the present reality can throw the midlife leader into a crisis. During these years it is easiest to let our guard down and decide that the race to the end just might not be worth it.

Looking at issues in the middle of life, Bob Buford challenges us to "go for the gold" in the second half of life, not giving up on our dreams and ambitions.

> The game [of life] is won or lost in the second half, not the first. It's possible to make mistakes in the first half and still have time to recover, but it's harder to do that in the second half. In the second half, you should at long last know what you have to work with. And you know the playing field—the world you live in. You have experienced enough victory to know how hard the game is most of the time, yet how easy it is when the conditions are just right.
>
> Some people never get to the second half; a good many don't even know it exists. The prevailing view in our culture is that as you close out your fortieth year or so, you enter a period of aging and decline. To pair age with growth seems a contradiction of terms. This is a myth I refuse to believe.[4]

Many people have accomplished great feats in their latter years of life. However, midlife is a time of soul-searching and also a time when we come face to face with the physical limitations of our own mortality. Our hair begins to fall out, our teeth give out, our bodies are slowing down, our shapes are changing, and we wonder if we still have the appeal and attractiveness we had in our youth.

Outward success can be our greatest enemy in the middle years. At this most successful time, we leaders are often the most vulnerable. If you read Gordon MacDonald's book, *Rebuilding Your Broken World*,[5] written after the great failure he faced in his personal life, you'll find he candidly describes the events leading to his own moral failure in the pastorate. His greatest enemy was the pressurized demands of his great success. He looked great on the outside but was decaying on the inside. Pressure stretched him too thin for his own good.

In a recent article MacDonald discusses what he calls "the seven deadly siphons" that cause us to lose enthusiasm for ministry as our spiritual passion runs dry. In my midlife experience I have struggled on each of these battlefields; what he is saying rings hauntingly true to life.

The Seven Deadly Siphons

1. Words without actions (talking a good spirituality without real-life practice in private).
2. Busyness without purpose (the lazy shallow river of busyness).
3. Calendars without a Sabbath (a filled-up calendar with no margin planned for quiet and reflection).
4. Relationships without mutual nourishment (acquainted with too many and intimate with no one).
5. Pastoral personality without self-examination (healing others without genuine self-evaluation).
6. Natural giftedness without spiritual power (allowing your natural gifts to carry you will eventually catch up with you as you run out of soul power).
7. An enormous theology without an adequate spirituality (a giant view of God and His work but a pea-sized personal spirituality).[6]

How do we push on to be effective in the middle years? What can we do to prevent the hollow drift into motion without inner substance? One answer is to refine our purpose and focus in life. In the second half it is imperative to write down your life dreams, your purpose, your mission statement. You may have done it early on in your career, but now in the middle years you need to take a hard look at the second half based on what you learned in the first. Peter Drucker points out things that will help in that pursuit: "*What have you achieved?* (competence). What have you learned that you are good at, and how can you build on your strengths to continue to contribute as a leader? *What do you care deeply about?* (passion). What is it that motivates you and satisfies you at the end of a week?"[7]

Buford calls this revised concentration the finding of the one thing in the box that you should focus on for your second half. Caring enough to keep going and growing in the second half takes more effort than in the first. Vaclav Havel said of this pursuit, "The real test of a man is not when he plays the role that he wants for himself, but when he plays the role destiny has for him."[8] Søren Kierkegaard said, "The thing is to understand myself, to see what God really wishes me to do . . . to find the idea for which I can live and die."[9]

The early years of our careers and ministry seem to be wrapped up in fulfilling other people's expectations.

Sooner or later a leader wakes up and realizes that he can never meet everyone's expectations and that he must quit worrying about what other people think.

This reminds me of what Bill Cosby says: "I don't know the key to success, but the key to failure is trying to please everybody."

Coming to this realization, a better approach is to (a) focus on what God wants as the ultimate contribution of my life, even if that means a radical change for my life, and (b) focus on what my relationship is with the most important people in my life: my Lord, my wife, my children. All those others who want a chunk of me come and go, but my personal relationship with God and my connection to my family is with me forever. Again quoting Bob Buford, "One of the most common characteristics of a person who is nearing the end of the first half is that unquenchable desire to move from *success* to *significance*. After a first half of doing what we're supposed to do, we'd like to do something in the second half that is more meaningful—something that raises above perks and paychecks into the stratosphere of significance."[10]

In thirteen years Peter Lynch took Fidelity's Magellan Fund from 20 million to 14 billion dollars. No one has had a more successful career on Wall Street. Yet at age forty-six he blew the whistle. His goal was to gain greater control over his own life. He explained, "My life was like a hot

fudge sundae: how much can you handle without getting a stomachache?"
He now stays at home each morning until the children are off to school
and works four days a week—two for charity and two for Fidelity. The
fifth day each week is spent with his wife!

Sure, you probably don't have responsibility for 14 billion dollars, but
Lynch's choice does provide a great lesson of looking at life in a fresh way
as we approach the second half of life. Although we may not have the
freedom to shorten our work schedule to one like Peter has, each of us
has the power to give our family more of ourselves and our time.

I began this section on the middle years with the illustration of running
the Vienna Marathon. I said, "Donna would not let me give up." That was
literally true! She and a friend took public transportation all over Vienna
(with our son in a stroller), literally chasing me by following a map I had
drawn with estimates of when I would be at various places on the marathon run. At each checkpoint, she would be waiting for me with cheers and
smiles and words of encouragement; then I would have a new burst of energy to keep going. Just as in that marathon, Donna in these middle years is
right there with me, cheering me on and believing in me. But beyond cheering me, she is an integral part of our team. Together, we are seeking to
navigate and finish well the marathon God has set before us.

THE MATURING YEARS

Prime Minister Golda Meir, one of the founders of the modern state of
Israel, once said, "Old age is like a plane flying through a storm. Once
you're aboard, there's nothing you can do."[11] But actually there is one
thing that can be done: *Don't give up.* It's never too late to get a new lease
on life. William James once stated that after age thirty people become set
like plaster, unwilling to change. But he is wrong, because many people
have made major contributions after age fifty. It was after age fifty that
Ray Kroc bought a couple of hamburger stands from the McDonald's
brothers. After age fifty Dwight L. Moody founded Moody Bible Institute, and after age fifty Billy Graham spoke to the most people ever at any
one time in his years of crusade evangelism.

One of America's most dramatic stories of starting life over again in the second half is that of John D. Rockefeller. At age fifty-three he was a miserable, paranoid billionaire. He was unable to sleep, felt unloved as a person, and lived in constant fear of his life. Having contracted a rare disease, he learned that the doctors had given up on him and said he had only a year to live. As he faced eternity and eternal issues, he decided to change his way of thinking about money. All his life up to that point he had hoarded money and his life was oriented inwardly. But then he established the Rockefeller Foundation and began giving away large portions of his money. His focus of philanthropy was on hospitals, medical research, education, and churches. Rockefeller received a new lease on his life, his health improved, and he lived to age ninety-eight. He went beyond selfishness and self-centeredness and began to focus on what he could do to help others.

The best way to view life in the maturing years of leadership is to focus in on the issues of finishing well. And this is a fitting conclusion to our study of effective leadership.

FINISHING WELL

"A tree is best measured when it's down." So goes an old woodsman's proverb. And how true this is of men and women. How will we know until it is all over whether they finished well?

In contrast to the failed voyage of the *Titanic*, a young "leader" that sank the first time out, there is a great warship of America's past that not only succeeded in all its dangerous voyages but was recently brought back to life after being out of commission for over a century. The *USS Constitution* ruled the seas for the United States Navy in the eighteenth century. No wonder, after being mothballed for over a century, the government poured millions into her restoration. This ship never lost a battle and went down in history as one of the navy's finest leaders. She finished so well they brought her back to life!

So in 1997 America's oldest battleship was relaunched. No living human being on planet earth had ever seen the *USS Constitution* sail, since it was drydocked 116 years ago. The scene can only be described as majestic, as this warship from a bygone era set sail from the Charleston (Mass.) Naval Yard. In the tradition of bringing back a bygone piece of American history, veteran news-caster Walter Cronkite became the official commentator of this cruise that took the newly restored and refitted two-hundred-year-old ship from Boston's outer harbor on a five-mile cruise off the coast of Marblehead. Twelve million dollars were spent to restore it, down to the finest detail. This was done to celebrate the two-hundredth anniversary of its original commissioning.

Old Ironsides, as the ship was affectionately known, was relaunched near its original launch site when it was first put out to sea in 1798. She was constructed of timbers felled from Maine to Georgia, armed with cannons, cast in Rhode Island, held together by copper fasteners made by Paul Revere, and, as such, is truly a national treasure.

Leadership is a lot like *Old Ironsides*. The apostle Paul was like that old ship—a survivor who was victorious in every battle he fought. He made it to the end, as recorded in one of the Scriptures' greatest displays of victory. The passion he showed toward the end of his life is compelling. On his way to meeting the fate that awaited him in Jerusalem, he gave a farewell speech to the Ephesian elders—a speech that summed up the passion of his heart. "And now, compelled by the Spirit, I am going to Jerusalem, not knowing what will happen to me there. I only know that in every city the Holy Spirit warns me that prison and hardships are facing me. However, I consider my life worth nothing to me, if only I may finish the race and complete the task the Lord Jesus has given me—the task of testifying to the gospel of God's grace" (Acts 20:22–24).

Then while in prison Paul wrote some of his most insightful and moving letters. In his letter to the Philippians, he shared the passion of his life that would not abate: "Brothers, I do not consider myself yet to have taken hold of it. But one thing I do: Forgetting what is behind and straining toward what is ahead, I press on toward the goal to win the prize for which God has called me heavenward in Christ Jesus. All of us who are mature should take such a view of things. And if on some point you think differently, that too God will make clear to you. Only let us live up to what we have already attained" (Phil. 3:13–16).

Even when in prison, Paul did not let up on his preaching. His readers may have reacted the way we should today. If he could have this kind of attitude in his prison cell, what is my excuse?

What will they say at your retirement party? What will your kids write on your tombstone? What will your friends remember about you?

The older I get, and the longer I watch the leadership game, the more concerned I am with simple fundamentals like finishing well.

I used to want to be a man known for great accomplishments—a person of notable deeds and ideas that rocked the planet. But now I would settle for this epitaph, "He was a good and godly man, loved his family deeply, and finished well."

The last couple of years I've spoken at retirement dinners for several individuals who have finished well. Each time I get this opportunity, my mind begins to fixate on this topic of finishing well. I've had the privilege in each of these instances to be able to say enthusiastically that the person has indeed finished well.

Recently a couple in their seventies (who could best be described as in their "convergence years") shared with some of our leadership team the lessons they have learned in their distinguished career in Christian leadership. As I introduced them, I admonished our young leaders to listen carefully to them. We've gotten hung up in our culture on worshiping youth and sidelining our elders. Somewhere along the way we have forgotten that eldership in the New Testament was connected to age. We can't go to a local Christian bookstore and buy the kind of wisdom that comes from years of experience. We can't download from an Internet site the maturity that can only be learned in the school of long and disciplined experience. How refreshing it was to have this couple in these final years of their active ministry share from their spiritual depths the lessons they've learned along the way on the road to spiritual resiliency. It was deep, rich, and satisfying. I think our young leaders at this seminar were surprised at how much they learned from these seasoned leaders.

There comes a time in every leader's life when he realizes it is time to back off. Moses certainly understood when it was time to pass the torch to Joshua. Though God clearly told Moses it was time for a leadership transition, the time is not always so clear-cut for us. Lyle Schaller says that most people stay in leadership positions too long, as opposed to leaving prematurely. A corollary to that principle is that if you stay too long, you can do more damage than if you leave too soon. We need to be sensitive to not overstay our welcome when it is time to step aside for the next generation or the next appointed person.

When it is time for transition in the leadership life cycle, it is important for all parties involved to deal from a position of grace and humility. I'll always be thankful to Warren Webster, whom I succeeded, for the gracious way in which he stepped down and made way for my presence in our organization. During the last two years of his leadership, especially when it became known that our board of directors had chosen me to succeed him, he did all he could to promote me and to step aside and to make way for me.

> *One of the great final acts of a good leader is to create a smooth leadership transition to his or her successor.*

Many leaders have failed in this critical final leadership challenge. They have been in control so long that it is difficult for them to give the reins to someone else. How could anyone possibly do as good a job or know as much as they do?

One way of knowing that it is time to step down is when you realize privately that you may no longer have what it takes to lead effectively. Keeping your job may be best for you, but you must ask, What is best for the organization? If you are a pastor, is it better for the church that someone else takes over who can take the ministry to new places, with different giftedness than your own? We need to approach our jobs from the first day we take over as a leader with the attitude that *we are not irreplaceable.* The cause can and will go on without us. While we are leaders, we want to make the maximum contribution and do the best job we can before the Lord. But when it is time to go on, we need to realize we are only humans and that God will raise up the next person in His time.

When we know it's time to leave and we can sense that our leadership contribution is winding down, we need to face that final transition head-on. In the spirit of Moses' passing the mantle to Joshua, we need to ask

God to give us the grace to bless and empower those who will follow us in leadership.

> Then Moses went out and spoke these words to all Israel: "I am now a hundred and twenty years old and I am no longer able to lead you. The LORD has said to me, 'You shall not cross the Jordan.' The LORD your God himself will cross over ahead of you. He will destroy these nations before you, and you will take possession of their land. Joshua also will cross over ahead of you, as the LORD said." . . . Then Moses summoned Joshua and said to him in the presence of all Israel, "Be strong and courageous, for you must go with this people into the land that the LORD swore to their forefathers to give them, and you must divide it among them as their inheritance. The LORD himself goes before you and will be with you; he will never leave you nor forsake you. Do not be afraid; do not be discouraged." (Deut. 31:1–3, 7–8)

We need to use grace and kindness as we relate to our older leaders when they reach the point in their lives where they are no longer effective. In their golden years they can make a great contribution in mentoring, counseling, writing, and teaching. That final transition is a move from direct leadership to indirect influence, or stated another way, from the work of doing leadership to the mentoring and sharing role of teaching about leadership.

The final stage of a life well lived for the Lord is what some call "the afterglow years." I like that term because it expresses the lives of leaders today like Billy Graham, Henry Blackaby, or Elizabeth Elliott, who glow in the fruit of a life lived in faithfulness to the Master. Paul had such an afterglow time during his last years in Rome while he was under house arrest. "For two whole years Paul stayed there in his own rented house and welcomed all who came to see him. Boldly and without hindrance he preached the kingdom of God and taught about the Lord Jesus Christ" (Acts 28:30–31).

IT COMES DOWN TO CHARACTER

In the introduction to the second edition of their landmark book, *Leaders: The Strategies for Taking Charge*, Bennis and Nanus observe, "Although a lot of executives are derailed (or plateaued), for lack of character or judgment, we've never observed a premature career ending for lack of technical competence. Ironically what's most important in leadership can't be easily quantified."[12]

Even these writers in the secular world know that character is a key issue for effective lifelong leadership. In fact they admit that the longer they study effective leaders, the more they have seen that character is the *defining* issue. Another person who has studied hundreds of leaders over a lifetime is Bobby Clinton. In his research he has found six barriers to finishing well.[13]

First, he says, is *finances*. As leaders grow in their influence and the amount of money they are responsible for, greed and mismanagement can easily creep in and compromise an effective leader. Examples are Gideon's golden ephod and Ananias and Sapphira.

Second is *power*. With the growth of power comes the subtle temptation to abuse it. Privileges come with a rise in perceived status, which can easily become abusive. An example is Saul's usurpation of the priestly privilege. Abraham Lincoln said, "Nearly all men can stand adversity, but if you want to test a man's character, give him power."

Third is *pride*. We must maintain a healthy respect for who we are and what we have accomplished, but we must not allow successes to go to our heads. God is the One who is to be given credit for anything good that comes from our ministries.

Fourth is *sex*. This one needs no elaboration and has been a key test of leadership from day one. Joseph did it right; David did it wrong.

Fifth is *family*. Tension and trouble in a leader's home can result in his or her ministry being destroyed. This can be between husband and wife, parents and children, or even between siblings.

Sixth is *plateauing*. Some leaders experience a growing dryness and dullness in their ministry. If this is not countered with a lifelong learning attitude and with spiritual renewal, plateauing will reduce the leader's effectiveness. This hardening can even lead to rebellion and disobedience, as in the case of Saul.

We've looked at the negatives; now let's focus for a moment on the positives. Again I am indebted to Bobby Clinton, who has done extensive research on leaders who finish well. In studying the lives of hundreds of Christian leaders who have finished well, he has isolated these recurring threads throughout all their lives.[14]

Leaders Who Finish Well

First, *they maintain a vibrant relationship with God.* Our relationship with God is first in our priorities for lifelong effective leadership. Accept no substitutes—they won't work.

Second, *they maintain a lifelong posture of learning and growing.* Leaders are learners. Never develop the attitude that you have arrived and that you can rest. Have the passionate attitude Paul had about maturity and Christlikeness, "This one thing I do."

Third, *they exhibit a Christlike character, the fruit of the Spirit.* Lifelong leaders who finish well exhibit the fruit of the Spirit throughout their lives. People who know them in private acknowledge that "what you see is what you get."

Fourth, *they live out their convictions in real life.* Effective leaders walk the walk; they don't just talk the talk.

Fifth, *they leave behind one or more ultimate contributions.* Those who have finished well have left behind a significant contribution to the church. It may not be known by others, but there is a lasting contribution to God's work.

Sixth, *they walk with a growing sense of destiny.* Those who make it well to the end have a sense of God's call on their lives throughout their lives. They are convinced that God has a plan for their lives, and they are determined not to falter in seeing that plan through to the end.

General Douglas MacArthur gave one of history's most famous retirement speeches at the end of his fifty-two-year military career. Speaking to the United States Congress on the day of his retirement, he bade farewell with these words:

"I am closing my 52 years of military service. When I joined the Army even before the turn of the century, it was the fulfillment of all my boyish hopes and dreams. The world has turned over many times since I took the oath on the Plain at West Point, and the hopes and dreams have long since vanished. But I still remember the refrain of one of the most popular barracks ballads of that day which proclaimed most proudly that 'Old Soldiers Never Die; They Just Fade Away.' And like the old soldier of that ballad, I now close my military career and just fade away—an old soldier who tried to do his duty as God gave him the light to see that duty. Goodbye."[15]

What a great way to finish well! There is nothing wrong with fading away into faithful retirement if you are able to look back and say, "I finished well." In his book *The Life God Blesses*, Gordon MacDonald has an excellent chapter entitled, "What Kind of Old Man Do You Want to Be?" Gordon's ten points of the effective older person are appropriate for this chapter on finishing well. Hopefully these ten will be the trademarks of all our lives in our older years: showing gratitude, having an enthusiastic interest in the accomplishments of the younger generation, keeping our minds sharp and agile, thinking in macroterms (seeing the big picture), never really retiring, still loving our spouses dearly, even romantically, not trying to hold on to institutional power, knowing how to pray, and not being afraid of death.[16]

One final thing to note about finishing well. We need to make sure our last will has a testament in it. Most people include in their wills only what actually is least important, the disposition of their earthly goods. Years ago people would actually take the time to make a testimony, and that old practice deserves a comeback. When your heirs sit together in the lawyer's office to hear the reading of your will, you will have one last opportunity to tell a captive audience what has mattered most to you in this life. Will it only include your jewelry, stocks, home, and savings? Or will you include something like this, which Donna and I have written?

Our Last Will and Testament

Of all the things we valued in this earthly life, our personal salvation in Jesus Christ was that of most value. Your mother and I met at Columbia Bible College, whose motto was, "To know Him and to make Him known." That is why we went to CBC, and had we not had that commitment we would never have met nor would we have become one in marriage and family. You, our children and grand-children, have grown out of our love and commitment to one another and our common bond in Christ. Our testimony is this, that Jesus Christ is the Lord and Savior of our lives. He is the heart of our family, and without Him we could have done nothing! Our greatest desire is that each of you will also know Him and allow Him to lead you all the days of your lives.

When we were married in 1975, at Judson Baptist Church in Oak Park, Illinois, we chose Ephesians 3:20–21 as our "marriage verse": "Now to him who is able to do immeasurably more than all we ask or imagine, according to his power that is at work within us, to him be glory in the church and in Christ Jesus throughout all generations, for ever and ever! Amen."

You would make us the happiest and most fulfilled if after we are long gone these words from the apostle John would ring true all your lives: "I have no greater joy than to hear that my children are walking in the truth" (3 John 4).

Much more could be said on this topic, which is as complex as the world in which we live. As we keep the main things the main things, the comforting thing to remember is that we serve the God of grace and mercy. He has chosen to use us, His imperfect vessels, in the great adventure of accomplishing His perfect will on planet Earth. To serve as a leader in that quest can be a profoundly rewarding pursuit.

ENDNOTES

CHAPTER 1—THE LEADER

1. A.W. Tozer, source unknown.
2. Ted Engstrom, *CEO Dialogues*, March 1993, 1.
3. Warren Bennis, *An Invented Life* (Reading, Mass: Addison-Wesley, 1993), xiii.
4. James Kouzes and Barry Posner, *The Leadership Challenge* (San Francisco: Jossey-Bass, 1987), 32.

CHAPTER 2—THE TASK

1. G. Frederick Owen, *Abraham to the Middle East Crisis* (Grand Rapids: Eerdmans, 1957), 45.
2. Ron Smith, letter to author, 28 February 1997 (italics his).
3. William B. Renner, quoted in Ralph Kilmann, *Beyond the Quick Fix* (San Francisco: Jossey-Bass, 1984), 92.
4. Johnny Miller, letter to author, 22 June 1997.
5. James Autrey, *Love and Profit: The Art of Caring Leadership* (New York: Morrow, 1991).
6. Peter Drucker, quoted in Olan Hendrix, *Christian Management Report*, February 1997, 10.

7. Alan Smith, letter to author, 5 March 1997.

CHAPTER 3—THE PERSON

1. Harry Truman, quoted in *Leadership 101,* ed. John Maxwell (Tulsa: Honor, 1994), 57.
2. John Maxwell, quoted in *Leadership 101,* 78.
3. John Wooden, quoted in *Great Quotes from Famous Leaders* (Lombard, Ill.: Celebrating Excellence, 1992), 77.
4. *Miriam Webster's Collegiate Dictionary,* 10th ed. (Springfield, Mass.: Miriam-Webster, 1997), 192.
5. Jerry Kirk, "A Way of Escape," *Leadership* (summer 1995): 88.
6. Steve Farrar, *Finishing Strong* (Sisters, Oreg.: Multnomah, 1995), 15 (italics his).
7. Gordon MacDonald, *The Life God Blesses* (Nashville: Nelson, 1994), 74.
8. Warren Bennis and Burt Nanus, *Leaders: The Strategies for Taking Charge,* rev. ed. (New York: Harper & Row, 1996), 154 (italics theirs).
9. *Miriam Webster's Collegiate Dictionary,* 608.
10. Bennis and Nanus, *Leaders: The Strategies for Taking Charge,* 42.
11. Douglas MacArthur, quoted in *Great Quotes from Famous Leaders,* 53.
12. Henry Blackaby, *The Power of the Call* (Nashville: Broadman & Holman, 1997), 14.
13. Richard Foster, *Celebration of Discipline* (San Francisco: Harper & Row 1978), 1.
14. Charles Haddon Spurgeon, *The Treasury of David* (McLean, Va.: McDonald, n.d.), 2:270–71.
15. MacDonald, *The Life God Blesses,* 42.
16. Ibid.
17. Billy Graham, *A Biblical Standard for Evangelists* (Minneapolis: World Wide Pictures, 1984), 74.
18. Billy Graham, "Standing Firm, Moving Forward," *Christianity Today,* 16 September 1996, 14–15 (italics his).
19. Charles R. Swindoll, quoted in Ben Winton, "America's Pastor," *Orange County Register,* August 1996.

CHAPTER 4—ENCOURAGEMENT

1. Donald Spoto, *Diana, The Last Years* (New York: Harmony, 1997), 76.
2. Phyllis Theroux, source unknown.
3. Ruth Bell Graham, quoted in *Topical Encyclopedia of Living Quotations*, ed. Sherwood E. Wirt and Kersten Beckstrom (Minneapolis: Bethany House, 1982), 65.
4. Hans Finzel, "Creating the Right Leadership Culture," in *Leaders on Leadership*, ed. George Barna (Ventura, Calif.: Regal, 1997), 272.
5. Charles M. Schwaabb, quoted in *Topical Encyclopedia of Living Quotations*, 66.
6. Bob Galvin, quoted in Mike Comerford, "Faces above the Crowd," *Chicago Tribune*, 1 February 1998, B1.
7. Hans Finzel, *The Top Ten Mistakes Leaders Make* (Wheaton, Ill.: Victor, 1994), 54–55.
8. Tom Peters, *Business Journal*, 9 September 1991, 24.

CHAPTER 5—CONFLICT AND CRITICISM

1. Abraham Lincoln, quoted in *Great Quotes from Famous Leaders*, 47.
2. Ken Williams, "Ten Biblical Ways to Diffuse an Attack," Wycliffe Bible Translators, 1 October 1996 (photocopy).
3. "What to Say When Two Members Won't Stop Fighting," *Practical Supervision*, 15 December 1997, 7.
4. James Emery White, "Be Honest about Myself," *Leadership* (winter 1998): 60.
5. Francis Schaeffer, *The Mark of the Christian* (Downer's Grove, Ill.: InterVarsity, 1975).

CHAPTER 6—VISION

1. Martin Luther King, Jr., quoted in *Great Quotes from Famous Leaders*, 43.
2. Eric Hoffer, quoted in Phillip V. Lewis, "Transformational Leadership," *Christian Management Report* (September 1997): 9.

3. Wally Scott, "Faces about the Crowd," *Chicago Daily Herald*, 12 October 1997.

4. James C. Collins and Jerry I. Porras, *Built to Last: Successful Habits of Visionary Companies* (New York: HarperBusiness, 1997), 91.

5. Leroy Eims, *Be the Leader You Are Meant to Be* (Wheaton, Ill.: Victor, 1975), 55.

6. "The Man Who Brought Marketing to Church: An Interview with George Barna," *Leadership* (summer 1995): 125.

7. Richard Beckhardt and Wendy Beckhardt, *Changing the Essence* (San Francisco: Jossey-Bass, 1992), 25.

8. George Barna, *The Power of Vision* (Glendale, Calif.: Regal, 1992), 28 (italics his).

9. Joel Barker, *Future Edge* (New York: Morrow, 1992), 28.

10. Aubrey Malphurs, *Planting Growing Churches for the 21st Century* (Grand Rapids: Baker, 1992), 234–36.

11. Burt Nanus, *Visionary Leadership* (San Francisco: Jossey-Bass, 1992), 3.

12. Finzel, "Creating the Right Leadership Culture," 272.

13. Stephen Covey, *The Seven Habits of Highly Effective People* (New York: Simon & Schuster, 1989), 101.

14. Bennis and Nanus, *Leaders: The Strategies for Taking Charge*, 89 (italics theirs).

CHAPTER 7—CHANGE

1. Niccolò Machiavelli, *The Prince*, trans. Henry C. Mansfield, Jr. (Chicago: University of Chicago Press, 1985), 23.

2. Finzel, *The Top Ten Mistakes Leaders Make*, 141–43.

3. Kouzes and Posner, *The Leadership Challenge*, 32.

4. Leith Anderson, "Ministry: Not the Same Yesterday, Today, and Forever" (St. Paul, Minn.: Bethel Seminary chapel message, 29 January 1996).

5. Stephen Covey, "Management Guru Lifts Up Humanity," *USA Today*, 27 October 1997, 8B.

6. Ibid.

7. Ibid.
8. Lewis, "Transformational Leaders," 10.
9. Machiavelli, *The Prince*, 23.

CHAPTER 8—THE LEADERSHIP TEAM

1. Theodore Roosevelt, quoted in *Leadership 101*, 27.
2. Bennis, *An Invented Life*, 107.
3. Bobby Clinton, *The Making of a Leader* (Colorado Springs: Navpress, 1988), 4.
4. Max DePree, *Leadership Is an Art* (New York: Dell, 1989), 14.
5. Warren Bennis, *Leader to Leader* (winter 1997), quoted in *NetFax*, 1 September 1997.
6. Lyle Schaller, *NetFax*, 8 December 1997.
7. Charles R. Swindoll, *Leadership: Influence That Inspires* (Nashville: Word, 1985), 56–57.
8. Bob Buford, "Important Lessons from Peter Drucker," *NetFax*, 7 July 1997.
9. Herb Kelleherm, "A Culture of Commitment," *Leader to Leader* (spring 1997, italics added), quoted in *NetFax*, 1 September 1997.
10. Jeff Bantz, "Generation X: Implications for Mission Organizations of the Sociological Distinctives of Christians Born between 1961 and 1975," *Impact Magazine* (summer 1997): 6–7.
11. Charles Arn, *The Win Arn Growth Report*, Issue 35 (Monrovia, Calif.: Church Growth, n.d.).
12. Leighton Ford, "A Letter to Future Leaders," *Christianity Today*, 11 November 1996, 16–17.
13. Ibid., 6–19.
14. Peter Drucker, quoted in *NetFax*, 7 July 1997.

CHAPTER 9—CREATIVITY

1. Karl Albrecht, *The Northbound Train* (New York: American Management Association, 1994), 138.
2. Barker, *Future Edge*, 80.

3. Henry Ford, quoted in *Great Quotes from Famous Leaders*, 19.

4. *Miriam Webster's Collegiate Dictionary*, 272.

5. Albrecht, *The Northbound Train*, 13.

6. Bill Hybels, "Finding Your Leadership Style," *Leadership* (Winter 1998): 84–89.

7. Jerry Rankin, "We Are Preparing Our Revolutionary Redesign," *Dawn Report* (August 1997): 9–11.

8. Percy Barnevick, foreword to *Leaders: The Strategies for Taking Charge*, x.

9. Bennis and Nanus, *Leaders: The Strategies for Taking Charge*, x.

10. Marcel Proust, quoted in Lewis, "Transitional Leadership," 10.

11. Kilmann, *Beyond the Quick Fix*, 92.

12. For an outstanding recent book on creativity in ministry, see Howard G. Hendricks, *Color Outside the Lines: Learning the Art of Creativity* (Nashville: Word, 1998).

13. Ann Landers, quoted in John Maxwell, *Injoy Life Club Notes* (San Diego: Injoy Ministries, n.d.).

CHAPTER 10—LIFE CYCLES OF LEADERS

1. J. Oswald Sanders, *Spiritual Leadership* (Chicago: Moody, 1969), 169.

2. Farrar, *Finishing Strong*, 8.

3. "Up & Comers: Fifty Evangelical Leaders Forty and Under," *Christianity Today*, 11 November 1996, 20.

4. Bob Buford, *Halftime* (Grand Rapids: Zondervan, 1994), 20–21 (italics his).

5. Gordon MacDonald, *Rebuilding Your Broken World* (Nashville: Nelson, 1988).

6. Gordon MacDonald, "The Seven Deadly Siphons," *Leadership* (winter 1998): 31.

7. Peter Drucker, quoted in Buford, *Halftime*, 123.

8. Vaclav Havel, quoted in Buford, *Halftime*, 23.

9. Søren Kierkegaard, quoted in Buford, *Halftime*, 61.

10. Buford, *Halftime*, 84 (italics his).

11. Golda Meir, quoted in *Great Quotes from Famous Leaders*, 55.

12. Bennis and Nanus, *Leaders: The Strategies for Taking Charge*, x.
13. Bobby Clinton, "Finishing Well: The Challenge of a Lifetime" (Pasadena, Calif.: Barnabas Resources, 1994), 8–9.
14. Ibid., 13–14.
15. Douglas MacArthur, quoted in Bobby Clinton, "The Mantle of the Mentor" (Pasadena, Calif.: Barnabas Resources, 1993), 1.
16. MacDonald, *The Life God Blesses,* 98–110.

BIBLIOGRAPHY

Adizes, Ichak. *Corporate Lifecycles: How and Why Corporations Grow and Die and What to Do about It*. Englewood Cliffs, N.J.: Prentice Hall, 1988.

Albrecht, Karl. *The Northbound Train*. New York: American Management Association, 1994.

Autrey, James A. *Love and Profit: The Art of Caring Leadership*. New York: William Morrow and Co., 1991.

Barker, Joel. *Future Edge*. New York: William Morrow and Co., 1992.

Barna, George. *The Power of Vision*. Ventura, Calif.: Regal Books, 1992.

————, ed. *Leaders on Leadership*. Ventura, Calif.: Regal Books, 1997.

Beckhard, Richard, and Wendy Beckhard. *Changing the Essence*. San Francisco: Jossey-Bass Publishers, 1992.

Bennis, Warren. *An Invented Life*. Reading, Mass.: Addison-Wesley Publishing Co., 1993.

————, and Burt Nanus. *Leaders: The Strategies for Taking Charge*, Rev. ed. New York: Harper & Row Publishers, 1996.

Blanchard, Ken, and Michael O'Connor. *Managing by Values*. San Francisco: Berrett-Koehler Publishers, 1997.

Buford, Bob. *Halftime.* Grand Rapids: Zondervan Publishing House, 1994.

Clinton, J. Robert. *The Making of a Leader.* Colorado Springs: NavPress, 1988.

Collins, James C., and Jerry I. Porras. *Built to Last.* New York: HarperCollins, 1994.

Covey, Stephen A. *The Seven Habits of Highly Effective People.* New York: Simon and Schuster, 1989.

De Pree, Max. *Leadership Jazz.* New York: Doubleday Dell Publishing Group, 1992.

Deal, Terrence E., and Allen A. Kennedy. *Corporate Cultures.* Reading, Mass.: Addison-Wesley Publishing Co., 1982.

Dyer, Charles H. *The Power of Personal Integrity.* Wheaton, Ill.: Tyndale House Publishers, 1997.

Farrar, Steve. *Finishing Strong.* Sisters, Oreg.: Multnomah Books, 1995.

Finzel, Hans. *The Top Ten Mistakes Leaders Make.* Wheaton, Ill.: Victor Books, 1994.

Flamholtz, Eric G. *Growing Pains.* San Francisco: Jossey-Bass Publishers, 1990.

Gangel, Kenneth O. *Team Leadership in Christian Ministry.* Rev. ed. Chicago: Moody Press, 1997.

Hendricks, Howard G. *As Iron Sharpens Iron.* Chicago: Moody Press, 1995.

———, ed. *A Life of Integrity.* Sisters, Oreg.: Multnomah Press, 1997.

———. *Color Outside the Lines: Learning the Art of Creativity.* Nashville: Word Publishing, 1998.

Kotter, John P. *Leading Change.* Boston: Harvard Business School Press, 1996.

Kouzes, James M., and Barry Z. Posner. *The Leadership Challenge.* San Francisco: Jossey-Bass Publishers, 1987.

Malphurs, Aubrey. *Values-Driven Leadership.* Grand Rapids: Baker Books, 1996.

Miller, Calvin. *The Empowered Leader.* Nashville: Broadman and Holman Publishers, 1995.

Nanus, Burt. *Visionary Leadership: Creating a Compelling Sense of Direction for Your Organization.* San Francisco: Jossey-Bass Publishers, 1992.

Sculley, John. *Odyssey.* New York: Harper & Row Publishers, 1987.

Tichy, Noel M., and Stratford Sherman. *Control Your Destiny or Someone Else Will.* New York: Doubleday & Co., 1993.

SCRIPTURE INDEX

SUBJECT INDEX